THE LIONS RAW

THE
LIONS RAW

A Captain's Story: South Africa 1997

MARTIN JOHNSON

WITH **HOWARD JOHNSON**

MAINSTREAM
PUBLISHING

EDINBURGH AND LONDON

Photographs © Fotosport

First published in Great Britain in 1997 by
MAINSTREAM PUBLISHING COMPANY (EDINBURGH) LTD
7 Albany Street
Edinburgh EH1 3UG

ISBN 1 84018 023 4

A catalogue record for this book is available from the British Library

Typeset in Adobe Garamond
Printed and bound in Great Britain by
Butler & Tanner Ltd, Frome

CONTENTS

ACKNOWLEDGEMENTS

I would like to say a big thankyou to several people who have been involved with *The Lions Raw*. First of all my thanks go to Howard Johnson, who did such a good job in his role as co-writer. I would also like to thank Bill Campbell, Cathy Mineards and everyone at Mainstream Publishing for their help with this project. Dave Gibson took some superb photographs for the book, for which I am very grateful, and I must also offer my thanks to the Lions' management team who did such a fantastic job on tour. Finally, of course, my thanks go to my team-mates in South Africa for their heroic performances. What a tour it was!

FOREWORD

It is with a mixture of pride and pleasure that I have written a brief foreword to Martin Johnson's reflections of the Lions Tour to South Africa.

Many people were surprised at Martin Johnson's selection as captain of the British Lions. With hindsight all of us can appreciate the wisdom of the decision after a highly successful tour. The type of rugby played was exciting to behold and proved that the northern hemisphere can produce a style of open running rugby and win matches with it.

Like many others I enjoyed watching the progress of the Lions Tour and I welcome the opportunity to thank the whole tour party and in particular Martin Johnson for his contribution.

My Company is the major supplier of Plaster Board Drylining Systems and Plaster within the UK and Ireland. As a market leader I have some understanding of the challenges and responsibilities of leadership. There are many styles of successful leadership and Martin Johnson demonstrated that by working quietly but effectively, coupled with leading by example on the pitch you can achieve remarkable results.

This is a thoroughly readable book, which, on behalf of British Gypsum, I am delighted to be associated with. I wish Martin Johnson every success in what should be a long career and I am confident that British and Irish rugby will prosper from the experience of this tour.

Paul Withers
Managing Director
British Gypsum Limited
(A subsidiary of BPB Industries plc)

CHAPTER ONE

Getting the Call-Up

To say that the news about the captaincy came out of the blue would be a lie. What wouldn't be untrue would be to confess that the way I got the news wasn't exactly how I'd expected it. The date was 28 March and I was in Gloucester preparing for Leicester's Pilkington Cup semi-final game against the local team. I'd been lying on my hotel bed getting some much-needed sleep before the big game. The phone rang and when I picked it up the voice on the other end said, 'I hear congratulations are in order now that you've been selected as captain of the British Lions for the forthcoming tour to South Africa.' I recognised the journalist's voice right away, but far from being delighted at the news he'd just given me, I was more annoyed. Annoyed at first because he'd disturbed an enjoyable bit of kip, then annoyed that he'd told me something – in a pretty smug tone, it must be said – that not even I knew officially. Captain of the British Lions. Even if it was true that I'd been selected for the job I certainly didn't want to discuss the matter with him, so I managed to get him off the line pretty quickly and then tried to go back to sleep. There were two or three journos who seemed to have a fast track to what was happening in the world of rugby union, their information usually turning out to be true, and this guy was one of them. But I wasn't going to give him a comment when the Lions' management hadn't even offered me the job and I certainly wasn't going to count my chickens. No. The best thing would be to put the issue to the back of my mind and prepare for the match against Gloucester in the best way I could think of. I rolled over and went back to sleep.

Leading the British Lions in South Africa was never something I'd planned for. After all, I wasn't even captain of England during the Five Nations series of 1997. I was more than happy playing my part in the England side under Phil de Glanville and was delighted to have been announced in the initial squad of 62 players, to be trimmed down to 35 at a later date, that Lions manager Fran Cotton and chief coach Ian McGeechan had drawn up for the summer tour. The players' names had been made public just after England had managed to defeat Ireland by 46–26 at Lansdowne Road in the Five Nations in what was an unprecedented move as far as the Lions were concerned. Never before had such a huge number of players been announced in a preliminary squad. Never before had so many rugby players been made aware so early that they were being considered for the most prestigious tour that any British or Irish player could hope to participate in. It was a clear signal that the management team for the 1997 Lions had their own ideas about how a tour should be run and that they weren't afraid to implement all manner of new ideas to make sure the tour would be a success. And that people had better get used to it.

That particular notion was only reinforced when the initial 62 players were called to a meeting at Birmingham's Metropole Hotel on 10 March, where Cotton and McGeechan would outline their plans for the eight-week tour. All the players were at the sharp end of their season, playing matches left, right and centre, but somehow we all managed to assemble to be addressed by the management and to see what we thought of the two men in charge of the tour. Ian McGeechan I knew as a good coach from my experiences with the British Lions in New Zealand in 1993, when I had been flown out as a replacement for Wade Dooley after he'd flown home following a family bereavement. I'd found 'Geech' straightforward and honest. When Fran Cotton had first been announced as manager, however, I must admit that I wasn't too sure about him. My initial thought was that he didn't have much experience managing an international team. He'd looked after touring sides for the North of England, certainly, but I hadn't played divisional rugby since 1993 and so hadn't had any contact with him at all. I'd never even met the guy. Of course, his reputation as a player and as a member of the legendary unbeaten Lions side to South Africa in 1974, went before him, and that earned him immediate respect amongst all rugby players. I also knew that during the previous season his forthright comments and opinions about the state of British rugby in general had seemed to be getting a lot of press coverage, but I hadn't spent a lot of time scouring the papers, keeping a close eye on the latest developments in what seemed like an ongoing series of problems at the RFU, so I couldn't make an honest appraisal of the man. I was intrigued to see what he would have to say for himself.

We all gathered in one of the meeting rooms of the hotel and Fran stood up to explain how the tour would work. He pointed out that the management team of 12 would be the biggest ever to leave the British Isles, but that he felt every member of that team was vital in order to achieve the main objective, which was to free the rugby players from any other worries besides playing – and hopefully winning – rugby matches. He then went on to tell us that unlike any other Lions tour to date there would be a 35-man squad as opposed to the more traditional 30 players, and he went on to outline how this would benefit the tour. Geech had spent two weeks with the New Zealand squad that toured South Africa with 36 players in 1996, watching and learning. He'd spent a lot of time with the Kiwis' coach John Hart, looking at how he'd organised his players, and had come to the conclusion that the All Blacks had revolutionised the way in which rugby tours took place. What Hart had done was effectively to split his whole party up, sending 21 guys around to play the midweek games and leaving the others to concentrate on the all-important Test matches. This seemed in many ways to be a brilliant idea, one which seemed so logical that it was amazing it hadn't happened before. If you played both Tuesday and Saturday games on a tour, naturally the early part of the week would be spent concentrating on the midweek game. If you only had a squad of 30 guys then at least six of the players involved in the Test team would definitely be sitting on the bench – which would hardly be ideal preparation for a big game four days later. Having a bigger squad, Fran argued, was the only way that a touring side could go abroad and stand a realistic chance of pulling off a Test series victory. It made perfect sense to me, although why he'd opted to settle for 35 Lions instead of a more logical 36-man squad (21 for each game including subs and 15 fresh players for the following game), I never found out.

Cotton then explained a little about the tour sponsors, the kit manufacturers, Adidas, and Next, the company which would supply all the squad's casual wear, and he showed us some of the gear that had been made for the players. The impression that he seemed to want to convey was one of organisation, quiet calm and authority, and I was impressed with the manner in which he made his points. Fran seemed to be very down-to-earth and straightforward.

Geech then stood up to make a few comments about how he wanted the Lions to play the game during the tour, explaining that Southern Hemisphere rugby was both faster and harder than we might be used to, and that if the Lions were going to be successful then we would have to match the Springboks not only in terms of pure strength, but also in the pace at which we would play the game. He left nobody under any illusions that it would be anything other than an immensely tough tour for the 35 who were eventually selected to go, but made it clear that he honestly believed that with the right amount of application the Lions would stand a great chance of winning the series.

In the hour or so during which the management team spoke, I was very impressed with their attitude and was already looking forward to getting involved in the tour if I was selected. To be honest, I thought it was very likely that I would get the nod. There had been rumours going around that I was one of the players under serious consideration to lead the party to South Africa, and this was confirmed when Fran came over and had a short word with me. 'You're on the shortlist for the captain's job for the tour,' he explained. 'How about if I call you later in the month and we'll have a chat to see what you think about it?' It was a bit of a tense moment, what with various other players standing around nervously, not knowing each other particularly well and not really knowing what to say. I felt awkward having the manager talking to me about the captaincy when there were other players within earshot, and I didn't want to hang around chatting with him like he was my best friend, giving the impression that the appointment was a done deal. I'd never even met Fran before, but the other players didn't know that, of course!

Naturally, I wasn't going to turn the job down. I couldn't imagine there would be any British or Irish rugby player out there who would, but there were plenty of other players in the frame. Ieuan Evans, Jason Leonard, Tim Rodber, Rob Wainwright and Lawrence Dallaglio were all guys whose names had been mentioned. I preferred not to think too deeply about the matter, though. I was just glad to be in the running, especially as my England captain Phil de Glanville hadn't even been named in the original squad of 62. I'm sure it must have felt like a slap in the face for Phil, as it would for anyone who thought they had a chance of being called up and yet didn't make it, so I wasn't going to take anything for granted. Besides, England had a game coming up the following weekend against Wales which I was supposed to be concentrating on, so once the Metropole meeting broke up the Lions went straight to the back of my mind. The season, both domestic and international, was coming to its climax and there were plenty of other games of rugby to worry about before South Africa would be uppermost in my thoughts.

I'd been reasonably pleased with my form throughout the season, one which had been as tough as any I've played in. It had been hard to bounce back from Leicester's Heineken European Cup final defeat against Brive back in January. We had genuinely believed we had a side that was a match for anyone in Europe, especially after beating Toulouse convincingly in the semi-final, but Brive had given us a real pasting, 28–9, playing a much quicker, more penetrative game that had really taken us apart. I'd never been so down after a game of rugby in my entire career, and I had joined up with the England squad for the forthcoming Five Nations game against Scotland not even feeling like playing, which had concerned me. It was only by the Thursday before the game that I felt truly motivated to take to the field again. My Leicester team-mate Graham Rowntree had said he felt exactly the same, and for the first hour against the Scots we didn't play at all well. Fortunately we came back strongly and scored 40 points, which gave me the lift I needed and got me back on track. Leicester started winning again, all my old enthusiasm started flowing back, and before I knew it we were in the semi-final of the domestic cup – and I was getting that journalist's call about the Lions' captaincy.

With such a lot of rugby still to play in the season I tried to put any thought of the British Lions out of my mind. I had two vitally important club matches coming up. There was the match against Gloucester which would end up putting us into the final of the Pilkington Cup after a 25–13 win. Then, a few days later, we met Wasps at home in an important league match. The day before the match, however, I called my parents at their home in Market Harborough and found out that another journalist had already been on the phone to them, asking for their feelings about my being selected as

Lions captain. The whole situation was rapidly getting out of hand, but there was very little that I could do except wait and see what developed. As it turned out, I didn't need to wait too long.

Fran phoned me at home in Oadby, a suburb of Leicester, on that Tuesday evening. It was April Fool's Day, curiously enough. The conversation lasted about 25 seconds.

'Martin, I'd just like to inform you that you've been selected to be captain of the Lions,' said Fran.

'Thank you very much,' I replied.

'I'll speak to you later in the week, then. Bye.'

Short and sweet, but a thrill nonetheless. I put the phone down, went into the living-room and told my girlfriend Kay that I'd been given the captaincy. She was delighted for me, but probably a little bit worried at the same time. She'd seen the enormous pressure that people like Will Carling had been under when he was captaining England, and she didn't fancy any invasion of our privacy. She's a rugby fan, comes to watch me when I play and is very aware of the rugby scene, so to a certain degree she was braced for this happening. I was pleased about the offer, too, but didn't go jumping about the place.

People have since asked me if I went out celebrating, but I don't think there's any point in celebrating before the job's done. I hadn't achieved anything yet. I suppose if I felt anything it was the responsibility that inevitably goes with the job. I was very aware that South Africa's a really hard place to go and tour, I had no experience as an international captain and precious little experience as a captain even at club level. I knew there would be a lot of attention focused on me and, yes, I wondered if I could actually do the job, whether I was big enough to take it on. You'd have to be a very, very confident man not to ask yourself if you were really up to it. I was also concerned about the press. Fran and Geech were quick to reassure me that they'd take some of the weight of dealing with the media off my shoulders (every player ended up attending at least one press conference on the tour), and I was pleased to hear that. I find the whole press situation a distraction on tour. I realise that you have to be media-friendly as a high-profile sportsman, but it's not my favourite part of the job. I don't mind sitting down and having a conversation about rugby if it's interesting, but most of the time you find that you end up saying the same things over and over again. In a press conference before a Test match you usually have to give five or six interviews where you're just repeating yourself, and the truth is I find it boring. I'm not going to tell the press the inside story, what's really happening in the camp, for obvious reasons, so unfortunately all I can do is trot out more of the same old stuff – which leads to a very unsatisfactory situation all round. But it was just something I'd have to live with, and, with the management's help, I decided that I'd be able to cope fine.

I gave my parents a ring to let them know I'd got the captain's job, and I phoned my agent, Darren Grewcock, to let him in on the good news. Darren had been telling me for ages that I was going to get the job, so he was saying 'I told you so' and enjoying feeling superior. Somebody must have told my Leicester club-mate Austin Healey what had happened, because he phoned me on my mobile impersonating Fran – and I actually fell for it, which amused 'The Dweeb' no end! That was it, though. No more larging it about the place. I just went for my usual couch slouch – the regular routine before a big league game – and plonked myself in front of the telly.

The official announcement of the 35-man squad for South Africa was made the next day, 2 April. I actually got my official letter in the post that day, which was both nice and unusual, considering that postal confirmation of being called up for any squad or team usually arrives three or four days after you've seen your name on Ceefax. I was asked to appear on a satellite link-up from the Leicester ground to the Sky television studios in London in the morning. Sky had signed an exclusive deal to broadcast all the Lions' matches live, so I went down to Welford Road with Eric Miller, Will Greenwood, Austin Healey, Neil Back and Graham Rowntree, the five other Leicester players who had made the touring party.

The Chief Executive of the Rugby Football Union, Ray Williams, announced the team from London and let the world know that I'd been chosen as skipper. It was great to hear the word officially being broadcast to the nation, but what gave me more of a thrill was seeing my mate Backy called up. He hadn't had a clue that he was ever in serious contention for the 35, having not even figured in the England set-up during the season, and he was absolutely shell-shocked by the news. Graham Rowntree had been pretty much certain to make the trip, Eric had pushed himself into the reckoning with some great performances, Will Greenwood, too, had played extremely well, but for me Backy's call-up was special, and I was absolutely delighted for him. It was nice, too, for me to know that there would be plenty of familiar faces around me on tour. I immediately thought that the Leicester lads would be very useful in sounding out what was going on with the players, what the mood in the camp was, especially during the tour's early stages. And all that sensible stuff aside, who wouldn't want their mates on tour?

The 34 members of the squad, myself excluded, were as follows:

Full-backs: Neil Jenkins (Pontypridd/Wales), Tim Stimpson (Newcastle/England)

Right wings: John Bentley (Newcastle/England), Ieuan Evans (Llanelli/Wales)

Left wings: Nick Beal (Northampton/England), Tony Underwood (Newcastle/England)

Centres: Allan Bateman (Richmond/Wales), Scott Gibbs (Swansea/Wales), Jeremy Guscott (Bath/England), Will Greenwood (Leicester/England A)

Utility Back: Alan Tait (Newcastle/Scotland)

Fly-halves: Paul Grayson (Northampton/England), Gregor Townsend (Northampton/Scotland)

Scrum-halves: Matt Dawson (Northampton/England), Austin Healey (Leicester/England), Robert Howley (Cardiff/Wales)

Loose-head props: Graham Rowntree (Leicester/England), Tom Smith (Watsonians/Scotland)

Tight-head props: Peter Clohessy (Queensland/Ireland), Jason Leonard (Harlequins/England), David Young (Cardiff/Wales)

Hookers: Mark Regan (Bristol/England), Barry Williams (Neath/Wales), Keith Wood (Harlequins/Ireland)

Locks: Jeremy Davidson (London Irish/Ireland), Simon Shaw (Bristol/England), Doddie Weir (Newcastle/Scotland)

Blind-side flankers: Lawrence Dallaglio (Wasps/England), Rob Wainwright (Watsonians/Scotland)

Open-side flankers: Neil Back (Leicester/England), Richard Hill (Saracens/England)

Number Eights: Eric Miller (Leicester/Ireland), Scott Quinnell (Richmond/Wales), Tim Rodber (Northampton/England)

I was generally very happy with the squad that had been chosen. It seemed to me that it was well balanced, with the right people chosen to fill the spots. I have to say I was surprised that Bath's Mike Catt hadn't been selected. He'd grown up in South Africa, knew the country and the style of rugby played there very well and was also versatile; he could play in any one of four different positions. There were also certain players who'd been selected whom I knew very little about. I had hardly come across Alan Tait or John Bentley during my time in the game, although I wasn't unhappy about their selection as I knew they were both strong and competitive guys from their days playing rugby league. Peter Clohessy was a bit of a surprise, having been playing his rugby so far away in Queensland, but again I didn't have any doubts about his ability, because to perform well in the Southern Hemisphere Super 12 tournament means you've obviously been doing something right. Some people made a few sarcastic comments about Peter's poor disciplinary record, but I wasn't too concerned about that. After all, I'd be playing with him, not against him. Finally, I wouldn't have known the hooker Barry Williams if he'd jumped out of my cornflakes, seeing as he'd only played once for the senior Welsh side.

I took all these offbeat selections as a positive move from Fran and Geech, though. It proved to me that the selection of players for the Lions party wasn't just following the usual tried and trusted formula of picking the guys who had done two or three good things in the preceding Five Nations tournament. In 1993 the Scottish forwards had performed particularly well against England at Twickenham and were duly chosen for the Lions tour to New Zealand, but this subsequently proved to be a very bad selection. The changes in the game since that time, especially with the advent of professionalism and competitive European club games, meant that it was now possible to see players performing in high-class games that weren't necessarily internationals. There was more good rugby for the selectors to watch, and they could get a more balanced impression of the players that way. Certain players might, after all, perform brilliantly wearing their country's jersey playing in front of a partisan home crowd; the whole emotion of the occasion might spur them on to almost superhuman achievements. That wouldn't happen in South Africa. We would need guys who could play well in the worst possible circumstances, not just the best. The selection of an uncapped player in Will Greenwood also made me think that the selectors had been thinking about what they were doing, rather than taking safe and easy options. It proved that they had firm opinions based on solid rugby judgement, and I thought that could only be positive.

Once the announcement of the squad and my appointment had been made on Sky, I had to undertake my first interview as Lions captain. It immediately gave me a good indication of the kind of questioning I'd have to put up with during the next three months. The first question I was asked was whether I was happy with the squad. What was I going to say? 'No, I think they're a useless bunch of rugby players and a real bunch of morons?' The second question that was put to me was whether I was at all concerned about my ability to handle all the speeches I'd be expected to make. I wasn't asked if I was worried about having to play three Tests against arguably the best rugby side in the world. Nor if I thought it was a tall order to also have to take on three Super-12 sides over in South Africa. Nor if it might be physically gruelling playing against powerful men like Mark Andrews and Kobus Wiese. No, surely my biggest concern had to be that I might make a cock-up of one of the speeches, of course! And if I didn't have them rolling in the aisles with my wit and repartee, then that would obviously make me a bad British Lions captain, wouldn't it? To be frank, I couldn't have given a toss about the speeches. If the Lions had wanted an after-dinner speaker as captain they could always have taken Peter Wheeler, because he's brilliant at it. The Leicester coach Bob Dwyer summed it up best when he was asked how I would handle the speeches and gave a terse 'Who cares?'. I couldn't have put it better myself.

What I was immediately thinking about was the job in hand. Playing for the Lions is special simply because it's such a rare event. There is only one tour every four years, and in many ways, because they only last seven or eight weeks, they're over almost before they've begun. The most important thing for me was making sure that representing the Lions wouldn't stop being special on this tour, because it had done in 1993 and the team ended up getting hammered in the midweek matches. A lot of people pay lip service to the honour that it is to represent the Lions. You hear players say 'It's the highlight of my career' time and time again, but the point is that you've got to make it the highlight. You can't just put the shirt on and think, 'This is it. I've made it.' If you go out and then get beaten 45–0, that's no highlight, that's just embarrassing. It's the quality of the individuals and their mental attitude that make tours and foster team spirit. When everyone goes into a tour with the right attitude, it makes it easier for all the squad members to stay on the right track. It's obvious a mile off if you're the one person out there who's slacking, and nobody wants to be that man. Fran and Geech obviously hoped they'd picked not only players with the right abilities, but players with the right mentalities. That, however, remained to be seen.

Leicester's league game against Wasps was played on the evening after the squad was announced and the side came home with a good 18–12 victory to keep us in the hunt for the championship. The schedule was beginning to get very hectic for most of the Lions players, and although Fran had originally set up a three-day meeting in Scotland for the 35 players between 13 and 15 April to have a couple of light training sessions and possibly organise the kit, it soon became clear that there was no way most of the players would be able to take that amount of time away from other commitments. The plan was scrapped. In the end it was decided that the only time all the players would be able to get together to get measured up and sorted out for kit would be on one single day, 21 April, again at the Metropole in Birmingham. There was very little contact between myself and Fran during the interim period. I was busy playing twice a week and Fran was obviously tied up with organising a million and one different things for the tour, so I don't believe I even spoke to him before Birmingham. I was sent a full itinerary, and although I knew the matches that we were scheduled to play, it was now that it first dawned on me how difficult a tour we were going to undertake. There were very few sides pencilled in for the midweek matches that could be classed as easy fixtures, and playing Northern Transvaal, Transvaal and Natal, three very powerful sides, within the space of a week looked like a tall order. I reasoned that if we were going to stand a chance in the Tests, then we might as well pit ourselves against the best of their provincial talent and hope that we could steer well clear of injuries. Whatever, the itinerary was set and that was the way things were going to be, so I just put it to the back of my mind for now.

CHAPTER TWO

Finishing the Season

Meeting up to get kitted out turned out to be quite good fun. I was the only member of the squad who'd already seen the stuff that had been put together for us. I have a sponsorship deal with Adidas and had already been to one of their sales conferences, helping them with the internal launch of the kit. I was very pleased with what they'd put together for us. I've been on more tours than you could imagine where the kits and the various bits of leisurewear are simply rubbish, and there's nothing worse than having kit where the training tops rip on the first day and casual clothes that the players think are disgusting and don't want to wear. That's when things accidentally get lost and the management then get pissed off with the boys because they look scruffy, while the boys are miffed because they didn't get what they wanted. It sounds like something and nothing, but, believe me, it makes a difference. If you look good then you feel like a professional outfit. Fran had been at pains to point out that this was going to be the first professional tour to South Africa, and it certainly seemed that the Lions were going to look the part.

Adidas had really put some thought into what we'd need and provided us with a bewildering but much-needed array of gear, from the usual T-shirts and sweatshirts to more 'exotic' stuff like flip-flops and beach towels. While they were taking care of the sports and leisure side of things, Next were measuring players for their casual and formal wear, the traditional blazer, trousers, shirts, ties, shoes and so on. It was a bit of a chaotic morning, but I actually thought it was good for the players to start getting to know each other in an informal atmosphere. I felt that it was important that I said hello to as many of the lads as I could, without coming across as this really over-the-top, back-slapping kind of bloke. I'd already decided that the best way to approach the job as captain was simply to be myself. I may not have known Jerry Davidson or Neil Jenkins particularly well – in fact, I didn't know Tom Smith from a hole in the head – but a lot of the 35 knew me pretty well from the England dressing-room and if I was suddenly to behave any differently just because I was the Lions captain, I think they would have thought I was a bloody idiot. And besides, if I'd thought it was a good idea to try and come across as having something other than my normal personality, I would soon have been found out. Nobody can keep up a false image over the course of an eight-week tour. The mask would soon start to slip and people would begin to see through you.

On a more serious note, I knew that I'd have to have a chat with Fran about a matter that had been concerning me. I'd been to Harley Street on 14 April to have a meeting with a top surgeon Dr Jerry Gilmore. He's a specialist in groin injuries and had actually successfully diagnosed one particularly troublesome groin injury that went on to be named Gilmore's Groin – in his honour, I suppose! I'd had a problem with my left groin since about February; it was nothing so serious as to stop me playing, but it was certainly causing me some discomfort. My physio down at Leicester had taken a look at it and thought it was a deep muscle strain. Gilmore, however, was fairly sure I'd need surgery to rectify the problem, but he was a big rugby fan himself and knew that I'd been picked for the Lions and obviously wanted to go to South Africa. He thought I'd be able to get through the tour on the proviso that I only played once a week. Now, of course, this bothered me. I was particularly worried that an injury that wasn't giving me too many problems on the softer English pitches might become a lot more troublesome on South Africa's notoriously hard playing surfaces. It never actually got to the point where I seriously believed that I wouldn't make the tour and would have to pull out, but I certainly didn't want to find myself in the situation where I needed so much recovery time that I wouldn't be able to train from, say, the Wednesday or Thursday before the Saturday game. Fortunately the press hadn't picked up on the injury, so there wasn't an extra pressure on me from that angle, but I didn't want to be over in South Africa as a lame or even half-fit captain.

I had a quiet word with Fran and explained what the problem was and he listened carefully as I told him about the advice I'd been given. He said that I should talk this through with the tour doctor, James Robson, who was also at the hotel, which I duly did. Dr Robson decided that all we should do was keep a close eye on the problem, and if the worst came to the worst then a cortisone injection would probably be sufficient to take care of things until I could have the operation back in London at the end of the tour. I was hugely relieved that everyone felt the same way about the damn groin and decided not to worry about it any more, at least not until it started giving me gyp again. And the sheer volume of games and the pressure we at Leicester put ourselves under at the end of the season was enough to keep my mind off the problem. Our final league game, on 3 May, was away at Sale. Our championship challenge had faded away by now and we could either save our season and qualify for Europe with a win or a draw, or lose and be without European rugby at Welford Road next season.

The atmosphere before the match was weird, unlike anything I've ever known. For the first time I realised that winning a game had become, not just emotionally, but financially important to the club. Without the extra revenue generated by European competition, Leicester would find the financial side of things harder, and so the pressure to win was definitely on; it was extremely important to come through. The match turned out to be tougher than anyone could have imagined. Sale blitzed us from the off and racked up a 13–0 lead which meant that we looked to be heading straight out of Europe. Tempers were running high and there was a tussle between myself and Sale's Charlie Vyvyan. A couple of minutes later there was a maul where one of our lads pulled Charlie out, and as he was being jerked away he turned awkwardly on his ankle and – so we thought at the time – twisted it badly. As he came out of the maul I dived in with a big hit. It was unfortunate timing, because after seeing me grappling with their player a couple of minutes earlier, as soon as Charlie went down everyone thought that my hit had broken his ankle, rather than the twist that had happened seconds earlier. He was stretchered off and the crowd began chanting 'Johnson Off' as if it were a football match. I didn't really mind – it was nice to have a crowd at all at Sale, to be honest – but the game got more and more nasty and in the end we pulled ourselves up by our bootlaces to earn a draw and a place in Europe. As I left the pitch the crowd were giving me a load of stick. I remember one guy in particular screaming: 'I hope you're happy now you've broken his ankle.' It was that kind of game. Our coach Bob Dwyer then got in on the act by having a bit of a barney with one of the Sale supporters while he was giving an interview for Sky and telling the bloke to fuck off live on air. It was a crazy game, but it was good to have achieved our goal.

Finally there was the small matter of the Pilkington Cup final the following weekend, again against Sale, to contend with. It seemed like everything had come to a head at once – the climax to the league, the Lions tour, the cup final, the groin problem – and I know certain rugby critics were saying that I would be exhausted at the end of a very demanding season for Leicester, maybe too exhausted for the Lions tour. Well, what was I supposed to do? Not go to South Africa? Not play for my club? Things were the way they were and I'd just have to get on with it. Which is what I did.

The match against Sale on 10 May turned out to be the highlight of what had been an exhausting season. We had Will Greenwood, one of our key players, back from injury, the game went well and we ran out reasonably comfortable 9–3 winners after a tough and competitive match. Pleased as I was to get my hands on the cup, I think my overriding feeling was actually one of relief at the end of the season. After all, before the Brive game we'd been in serious contention for three trophies. I was really worried that the whole season would go sour and that we'd end up with nothing, especially because we'd been playing so much rugby and I knew we were all very tired and probably losing our edge. On top of that, my girlfriend Kay and I had just moved into a new house in a tiny, picturesque village outside Leicester, which had also been a hassle. We'd moved all the stuff ourselves. My Leicester team-mate Matt Poole owns an office furniture business and he lent me one of his vans to help with the move. It only took a couple of trips and we were only moving five or six miles, but it was hard graft all the same. The place was gorgeous and we were both very excited about getting in there, but the move hadn't come at a great time. I thought it would make me even more knackered. As it turned out, though, by the time I set out for the Oatlands Park Hotel in Weybridge on the Monday morning two days after the cup final to meet up with the Lions party, I was feeling fairly refreshed and ready to get stuck into the challenge of a very exciting tour.

CHAPTER THREE

Oatlands

As I drove down from Leicester with Graham Rowntree in my Ford Scorpio, I was beginning to get excited at the thought of the forthcoming eight weeks. I enjoy driving the Scorpio, even though everyone else thinks it's the most hideous car ever, but it suits me. It's big, ugly and slow!

We pulled into the hotel at 12 noon. 'It's just like turning up for your first day of school,' said Graham, and he was absolutely right. When you meet up with a new bunch of guys, you're always out of the comfort zone that you build around yourself at your club. Even with England I've been around so long that it feels like home, but the Lions was something different. Oatlands is a beautiful hotel with massive grounds to help you feel like you're really getting away from things. I'd never stayed there with England, but apparently the Lions have often used the hotel in their build-up to tours and I believe a lot of sides touring over here stay there. It's close to London, but not too close, which may well be part of the appeal. It seemed like a great place to chill out, but I was a bit concerned that the work we'd be doing in this week before we left might be physically demanding and very draining. I'd spoken to Geech in Birmingham about what he had in mind for us at Oatlands, and he'd said that he knew everyone would be knackered at the end of their domestic seasons and that the week wouldn't simply be hard graft, or hard yakka as Bob Dwyer loves to call it; there'd be plenty of other activities for us to get involved in. He was only intending to have three, maybe four rugby sessions, and was more concerned about getting the players into the right way of thinking. I was impressed by what Geech had said because again it showed that he was really aware of the players' needs and was actively doing something about it. I just hoped he'd be as good as his word.

As things turned out, I needn't have worried. The whole time we spent at Oatlands was very well thought-out. There weren't many other guests at the hotel, which meant we pretty much had the run of the place. As we sat down for lunch on that first day I felt that there was a certain atmosphere in the air, that the various nationalities were sticking together a bit and that nobody was mixing. I wasn't too worried about that, though; I thought it was only natural and that the barriers between players would be broken down quickly enough. I sat with some of the Welsh boys and tried to indulge in some polite conversation, which I reckoned was something I should do as captain.

The first meeting of the squad took place in a room which was too small, too hot and too cramped. It wasn't the most comfortable of environments for Fran to give his first speech on the tour proper, but that was the way things were and he just got on with it. Without getting too sergeant-majorish about things, he explained in no uncertain terms what we had let ourselves in for on this tour. It wasn't anything that we didn't already know, but he drilled the idea into us that this would be an incredibly hard tour and that if we were to be successful then there were certain basic things that we needed to do and certain ways that we would have to behave. Fran insisted above all that there would be no cliques. They had formed in 1993 and it had turned out to be a real problem. He was adamant that there was no such thing as a Test side that was already picked, and that the team to play South Africa would be selected on the strength of people's performances on the tour and on those performances alone. We were all in this together, and if we could engender that spirit quickly and build on it then he really believed we had a chance of beating the 'Boks. There would be no slackers, everyone would know exactly where they stood and we would work to get the focus right. Fran was also at pains to point out that while we would be down in South Africa on business, for want of a better word, the management was not there to act as our guardians. All they wanted was to take care of everything to leave us free to play the best rugby of our lives. I thought it was another good speech and so didn't feel the need to stand up and say anything myself. What else could I add?

Geech got up and said a few words about the rugby side of the tour.

He was particularly keen to emphasise the fact that what he'd been trying to achieve when he picked the squad was to get the right players in the right place at the right time. Timing was all-important, and to that end he expected everybody to understand the importance of being on time throughout the tour. If people were kept hanging around for hours on end then it did nothing for team spirit, and while that might sound like a petty point, he assured us that it would become a problem if we didn't take care over punctuality.

Again, I liked the way Geech put his points across. While some people are more into having a giggle on tour than others, the bottom line, as far as I'm concerned, is that you're out on tour with only one aim: to win the Test series. You're not out there to have a laugh at the expense of the rugby. Anyway, I couldn't see how you could have fun on tour if you weren't focused that way. My idea of having fun was winning those Test matches; that was my idea of a good time. I've always believed that if you're successful on the pitch, then the other business will take care of itself and you'll have a happy touring party. If you start losing, then the whole mood of the party plummets. If you're on a winning streak, the press leave you alone, guys who are out of form find themselves getting dragged along and things start to roll. It seemed very obvious to me. If you're going to be a Lion you might as well go out there and try to be a successful one. Going to South Africa was a great opportunity and to my mind there was absolutely no point in going out there and doing things half-heartedly. I think everyone knew that if we didn't play well against the Springboks then we'd simply be blown away. The only way we'd stand a chance would be if we stuck together.

I knew it would be really tough, but I also genuinely believed that if our attitude was right, we could certainly compete. I didn't care that the press thought we didn't stand a cat in hell's chance against the Springboks, because how often do the sports press really know what they're talking about? I'd weighed up the fixtures that we had to play and I could see us losing some of the provincial matches – we were playing good sides. But if we didn't get down about that and hit the Tests with everything we had, then we were definitely capable of winning. Everyone was blathering on about how great the South Africans were, but, don't forget, they'd lost to France in 1993, drawn with England in '94, won the World Cup in '95 on the back of a huge wave of emotion and lost to New Zealand in '96. The evidence suggested that they were beatable. Of course they had great players and of course they were very physically intimidating, but those were things you had to deal with. I was confident that the players the management had chosen could certainly match the Springboks' physicality and if we got off to a good start, then anything was possible.

I was slightly surprised by the fact that the first meeting had turned out to be quite heavy, considering it was the first time we'd all been in a room together. It definitely gave us plenty to think about, but the atmosphere soon lightened when we were told that the next thing we needed to do was to go round to see the tour doctor, then Adidas and Next, to have a check-up and pick up our gear. The tour's baggage master, the appropriately named Stan Bagshaw, was in charge of organising everything, so split us into three groups, A, B and C. This was the first time I'd seen Stan in action, but he got things off to a flying start by saying two groups should go round so the rooms wouldn't get too crowded. Great idea, until you realised that this meant one group would be sitting on their arses doing nothing. The whole place fell about when they realised just how ridiculous Stan's instructions were, but he couldn't have broken the ice any better if he'd plotted his speech meticulously.

The doctor's check-up proved to be a pretty standard affair: teeth check, weight analysis, fat test and a general medical to make sure that the knees were okay and there weren't any hernias appearing. The Next clothes were a little more problematic. It appeared that there had been a few problems with the measurements, so some people had collars that were way too small for them while the sleeves of their jackets were halfway up their arms. It was chaos, with trousers, jackets, shoes and belts strewn all over the place like the first time we'd been sorting out kit in Birmingham, although no one was getting too stressed about it. Far more interesting, however, was picking up the kit that Adidas had made for us. There was tons of it, but the problem was that it was crammed into just two sports bags, a feat that was achieved with the kind of neat packing of clothes that only your mum knows the secret to. No man in the history of the universe has ever packed a bag like that! It was obvious that we'd be needing a load more bags, and, to give Adidas their due, they sorted it out. They also gave the lads a very nice watch each, which was a thoughtful gesture.

Of course, sponsorship in sport these days is big business and we were all aware that it was important to wear the right gear. The rules are well defined. Your footwear can be manufactured by your own personal sponsor if you have one, but you're not allowed to wear any branded clothes from companies other than the official sponsor. You can't go training in any old gear, otherwise there'll be hell to pay. You even have to tape over any other sponsor's logo you might have on your Lycra shorts. It can be a pain sometimes, but you soon get into the habit of wearing the right gear. It's going to be second nature to rugby players before too long, and it's a small price to pay considering the benefits that sponsors have brought to the game. People ask me whether having to give TV interviews wearing a baseball cap advertising something or other isn't just a little bit annoying. The answer is 'Not really'. It's no big deal and you just get on with it. I was invited down to the British Grand Prix qualifying day last year as a guest of Tyrell and I was allowed into the pits while the technicians were working. It was incredible, but it seemed that nobody was allowed to tell me to get lost and get out of the way, presumably because I was with the paymasters. That's just the way of things, I suppose, although I find it hard to believe that there could be a load of people milling around the England dressing-room at Twickenham five minutes before the start of an international in the future. Who knows for sure, though?

Our first full day at Oatlands began with our first session with the management training company Impact who had been hired for the week. One of the guys from the company started off by trying to explain what the objectives of these sessions were: to teach everyone about themselves and their team-mates and to help us all learn how to communicate with each other better, to trust each other and to think as a team, rather than solely as an individual. I wondered how much of this stuff the lads would take on board. I wouldn't have been at all surprised if they'd been very cynical about it, but to their credit they responded really well and put a lot of effort into the sessions. I think we all reaped the benefits of that positive attitude because the Impact sessions turned out to be a lot of fun.

The whole of the party, management included, were split into groups of seven to do a series of exercises. I remember hooking up with Allan Bateman in my group for the first exercise, which was probably the weirdest of the lot. We had to stretch our arms out so that our fingertips were pointing straight out and flat at shoulder height. The idea of the exercise was to balance an ordinary piece of garden cane on our fingers and, without anyone's fingers leaving the surface of the cane, simply to put it on the floor. I wouldn't be at all surprised if you think that sounds incredibly easy, because so did I. Getting the damn cane down proved to be a lot more difficult in practice, though. You get so paranoid as soon as anyone's fingers look like leaving the cane that people automatically overcompensate. No matter how hard you try, the cane starts to go up instead of down. I could see the cane going up right before my eyes, but I still couldn't believe it was happening. I was convinced that someone was messing about; it was freaky. In the end people would be trying to cheat, holding their thumbs over the cane to force it down. It made us realise that communication between team-mates is not always as simple as you believe it is, and nor is teamwork.

Next, we went out into the hotel grounds and were shown two poles stuck into the ground about ten feet apart. Between the two poles were pieces of plastic tape randomly arranged and criss-crossing so that the effect was like a spider's web. What we were asked to do was to get all the members of the team through a different hole without touching the plastic tape. Of course, some of the holes were large and easy, while others were small and difficult, and the idea was that we all had to get used to problem-solving together. We had to think and plan things through before we dived into action. Guys were being picked up and passed through holes high in the air and we had to make sure that there was an easy hole left that the last guy could get through on his own. We managed it pretty well, which told me that our group had good organisational and communication skills. The whole thing was good fun and got the guys into the Impact sessions from the off. If they'd been worried about really being put through their paces on the rugby training pitch, then this seemed like a much more pleasant alternative, and it got all the players in a really good mood.

Right from the start of our Impact sessions we had to get used to the idea of having a TV crew around. I found out later that the idea was to film a documentary of the entire tour to give viewers a unique insight into what it's really like on a Lions tour. I was a bit dubious at first. I wasn't too keen on having a lens poking its way into everything that was going on, and I could see a lot of potential problems if things started to go wrong when we were out in South Africa. To be fair, the lads in the crew were very good. They were very careful not to be in the wrong place at the wrong time and accepted that the players would be bound to get upset with them if they got in the way of their work. They were very keen to emphasise that they wanted to work with us, rather than try to catch us out and upset us. I think they played their cards right from the off. If we asked them to turn the cameras off then they did it without arguing the point, which went down well. In the end it was very rare that this ever happened, and most of the time the players didn't even notice them around. The worry with these kind of documentaries is that you can do all kinds of things editing a film that can change the sense of what was happening at the time and it's not very difficult to make people look bloody ridiculous. It's difficult to catch the atmosphere in a room on film, so that you might have 21 guys sitting in a very intense team meeting which actually comes out on film as 21 boring blokes looking bored. I haven't seen the results of what they shot yet, so I can't comment on how successful this particular film is, but I hope it gives people the right impression of what being on the tour was like.

In the evening I had my first tricky problem to deal with. There was a discrepancy with some of the boys' tour insurance; either they were underinsured or there was some conflict between their club's insurance and what they were insured for on tour, I can't remember now. I had to go and try to get a suitable deal organised so that if anything career-threatening happened to one of the guys during the tour then they would be adequately taken care of. I didn't particularly like having to deal with the negotiations with the management, but that was one of the responsibilities I'd taken on when I accepted the captain's job, so I just got on with it and we came to an arrangement that everyone was happy with, which was a relief. I could relax and spend the end of the day listening to the Chairman of the Four Home Unions Committee, Ray Williams, giving us a speech, the usual kind of geeing-up stuff. By the time I went to bed, I felt I was already well into the spirit of the Lions and that things seemed to be coming together nicely.

9.15 on the Tuesday morning saw us all on the coach heading for the London Irish ground for our first British Lions training session. Every morning during the tour the administration assistant Sam Peters gave everybody a printed sheet with the activities for the forthcoming day printed on it. It might sound a bit childish, giving grown men a set of instructions in this way, but I was all in favour of it, as nobody had an excuse to be late for anything.

The session turned out to be fairly light – a bonus, because I'd been expecting hard yakka in this first session. Dave McLean, our fitness adviser, was given the task of warming us all up with some light jogging, which is pretty standard practice. The problem was that instead of having us jog around the edge of the pitch like just about every club in Britain does, Dave had us doing what could only be described as 'formation jogging', trying to keep in a straight line together, then all going right or all going left. No one had a clue what he was on about and for the first ten minutes you had the sight of hardened, top-line rugby players crashing into each other and generally making a right cock-up of things as we tried to get things right. I was annoyed by the whole affair; there we were trying to get a good session in so that we could try to get to know each other's styles of play and all the rest of it, and all we were doing was pissing about trying to warm up. I could just see eight weeks of formation running stretching ahead of me!

The jogging fiasco didn't get the training session off to a good start and things were generally pretty sloppy. Mark Regan managed to bowl our assistant coach Jim Telfer over from two yards with an unintentional hit which sent Jim absolutely flying, glasses in the air. No one really knew how Jim would react to being pummelled by a hooker in full flow, but he didn't want to show that he'd been hurt and took it quite well. The ball was going to ground far too much and it was also fairly clear that one or two of the boys weren't fully fit. Paul Grayson and Will Greenwood looked like they were carrying knocks and Peter Clohessy was really struggling. He couldn't even run properly, trailing a leg behind him in a very ominous fashion. At the end of the session Fran and Geech came over and told me what I'd already worked out: that Clohessy wouldn't be getting on the plane. There wasn't much you could say to the fellow, so back at the hotel after training I had a quiet word with him and told him I was sorry he wouldn't make the tour and that was effectively that. One day into the tour and one guy down. To be honest, I believed that we'd lose at least one more before we left on Saturday. It had been a long, hard season. It was decided that Paul Wallace would be called up to the squad as Peter's replacement.

On the coach on the way back to the hotel from the first training session one or two of the boys were moaning about the schedule that had been arranged for them. It looked like we would be working till late on most days and there would hardly be any relaxation time, so I had a chat with Fran and Geech and managed to get them to give the lads Thursday afternoon off. I was pleased for two reasons. First, it proved that the management were prepared to listen to what the players had to say and to act on it. And second, it was good that I'd managed to act on behalf of the players and get a result.

After dinner on Tuesday we had our first session with Andy Keast, who had taken on the role of technical coaching assistant. Andy used to be director of coaching at Natal between 1994 and 1996 and had even led them to a Currie Cup win against Western Province in 1995, so his credentials for analysing the South Africans were second to none. Keasty must have spent half the tour watching videos of rugby games and started off that night the way he meant to go on. I don't have Sky television at home, so hadn't watched any of the rugby played in the summer of '96 when the Springboks had met New Zealand. I'd wanted a break from the sport, to be honest, but Graham Rowntree had seen all of it and had told me that the South Africans were playing rugby which was possibly better than that which they had been playing when they had won the World Cup the year before. I knew they were a great side, but I wasn't particularly aware of that many individuals, so Keasty's work was very useful and interesting to me. He explained how the 'Boks played a hard, pressing game and how we could hope to combat it, picking out their key players along the way. He showed us quite a lot of footage of Natal, especially the fly-half Henry Honiball, whom he obviously rated highly. It was obvious that he had a lot of respect for what the South Africans were capable of doing on a rugby field and it was a sharp reminder as we all went off to bed that this tour wasn't going to be any kind of holiday.

Wednesday 14 May began at 9 a.m. with another of our Impact sessions, this time canoeing on a local river. I was in a three-seater with Tom Smith and Richard Wegrzyk, the tour masseur, which turned out to be good fun. We managed to complete all the tasks given to us by the people running the session without falling in the water, which was a good effort on our part. I enjoyed myself, much more so than in the second session of the morning where the exercise was to set up a rope and pulley type affair over the bough of a tree and build a tower of beer crates with one person sitting on top of them. It was all about building your teamwork skills, but my head for heights isn't all that clever and I wasn't unhappy to fall off with the beer crate total at 15. Tom seemed happy as Larry up there and managed to perch on top of 25 crates. Good luck to him. I wasn't competitive enough to want to beat him!

After lunch and another speech, this time by one of the girls from Scottish Provident, we headed out for our second training session, which turned out to be much more physical than the first. There was a lot of hitting bags and generally working up a sweat and getting into some hard work. John Bentley was already beginning to come into his own as a tour character, shouting away and encouraging everyone to get into it. I was a little bit wary of the guys who had played a lot of league, purely because I thought they might be used to a different way of doing things that they would think was better, but there was never any bother. Everyone seemed to enjoy themselves and got a buzz out of working hard. I was very pleased with the way things had gone and afterwards made a little speech as captain. 'We've set ourselves a very high standard with the effort we've put in during today's session,' I said. 'We mustn't let that level of commitment and work-rate slip from here right through to the end of the tour.' It felt right to say something at that point and the guys responded positively. It seemed I wouldn't have any problems with keeping people motivated; everyone seemed determined to do well and not let themselves or anybody else down.

Returning to Oatlands we immediately had to get changed into our Number Ones (that's the blazer and slacks routine) for the official team photograph. The alterations which had been necessary had been made to the blazers, but the shirts hadn't come back yet, so Stan Bagshaw was quickly dispatched to High and Mighty in London to get the necessary replacements, otherwise the team photo would have looked like something out of a comedy movie. Poor old Stan. 'See Stan' was already becoming the tour battle-cry when anything didn't go exactly to plan, and that didn't change for the rest of the time we were together.

The traditional farewell dinner for the squad took place that evening at the Café Royal in London. I'm not mad keen on this type of function. You end up sitting at a table full of people you don't know and as the evening wears on they tend to get more and more drunk and rowdy, whereas you're on your best behaviour, which isn't too much fun. The more people had to drink at the Café Royal, the more emotional everyone became. Everyone was coming up and wishing me luck, which was nice but eventually tiresome, and one old boy even shook my hand until I thought it was going to come off while saying 'God bless you' to me very sincerely. It was too early in the tour to be thinking about what other people's expectations of you might be, but I could already tell that a lot of the people wishing me well here would be on my back once we were out there if things weren't going well. I take the whole hoopla with a pinch of salt. Of course it's nice when people are wishing you luck, but you do tend to get asked the same inane questions, to which you give the same inane answers. 'What do you think the tour will be like?' 'Well, it'll be tough.' 'Are you going to win?' 'Well, we'll certainly be doing our best.' What do they think I have? A crystal ball? You're always on a loser at these dos. If you're not the most charming man who ever walked the earth to everybody you talk to, then they think you're some kind of big-headed idiot. You can't win. To be honest, I was glad when we got out of there and even happier when we were given an extra half-hour's lie-in before we had to get back to work on Thursday morning.

The following day's Impact session concentrated on how to deal with the media, something that I obviously paid particular attention to. Part of my job as captain revolved around speaking to the press and it was something I'd have to get used to. I also knew there'd be a lot more focus on this tour than ever before and with it came certain responsibilities. The minute big blokes start running around hotels and messing about, then damage is pretty likely to happen. If you don't manage those situations carefully, then the press can soon have you written off as drunken vandals. The old Lions tales of on-tour madness are very funny (at least, if you're not a hotel owner they are) but the increased media profile meant that we wouldn't be able to get away with that kind of behaviour. The '68 Lions once threw a bed out of the top-storey window of a hotel to see what would happen because they were bored. Imagine if that had happened in '97! On one tour in New Zealand someone had a room above the hotel bar, so they turned the taps on and then took bets downstairs as to how long it would be before the water started seeping through the roof of the bar. I didn't think we'd be able to get away with that kind of stuff any more, and Impact confirmed it in their presentation.

Do I miss the boozing and high jinks? Not particularly – and certainly not enough to end up in the tabloids because of it. I'm waiting for the first tabloid exposé of a senior rugby player, because it really can't be far off now. The way things are at the moment all sportsmen are fair game.

Does that mean that I'm always going to be bland for the papers and TV? I'm not really sure. I try to say what I feel without being controversial for the sake of it. I don't want to be stirring things up in the press, because that's not my style. I never tried to bait the South Africans through the papers because I thought that would simply be giving them ammunition with which to build themselves up to play us; psychological warfare isn't something I'm particularly interested in. I don't like to see 'Johnson says this' or 'Johnson says that', because I know that the papers are always looking for their little angles. I'll always try and answer questions intelligently, but I know that people aren't really interested in rugby talk, but in scandal. The kind of stuff that's interesting to the papers is always the kind of stuff that I think you have to say to someone face to face. Why air your dirty laundry in public? It's not that I don't like to talk. There's nothing I enjoy more than sitting around nattering with the lads. I'm just wary of what the press can do to you, and I treat them with caution.

If I was sceptical about the press, I had good reason to be guarded during the media gathering at the hotel at midday. I'd never seen so many TV cameras reporting on a rugby event before and it suddenly hit me how much interest there was in what we were doing. I'd say that this conference made me more nervous than any other one on tour. It was the first time that I had to sit in on a conference as Lions captain and all the lads were present as well, circling like sharks, waiting for me to say something stupid! I was lucky, to be honest, because some of the toughest questioning was directed at Fran, asking him whether his ongoing battles with the RFU would prove to be a distraction from managing the tour. I think he was a bit taken aback by the line of questioning, so I tried to step in and talk more about the rugby. It wasn't a particularly pleasurable experience, especially when our press co-ordinator Bob Burrows introduced me as 'The Lion King'!

The whole affair proved to be pretty tiring, and there was no relief after the conference as I was shunted about doing one-to-one interviews and photos. Photos are actually the worst thing of all, because people are always looking for you to do something stupid. Naturally someone had brought down a huge cloak and a crown for the 'Lion King' shot, but that was a bridge too far and I told them they hadn't got a chance of me posing like that. The lads would have killed me!

The demands on everybody's time were already proving to be massive as Mark Regan, Lol Dallaglio, Austin Healey, Simon Shaw and I left for London and the RFU Awards Dinner in London. I couldn't help wondering how I was going to be able to put up with this for two months. It wasn't a bad do, to be fair, even though the seating arrangements were quite embarrassing. All the tables were round except for one long one in the middle of the room, which was where the Lions were all supposed to sit. The trouble was that only about five of us had turned up and when we were introduced and asked to stand up it looked like a bit of a spartan showing. We had a bit of fun with the Wasps lads who were there celebrating their league championship win, and Austin won an award for Try of the Year for his effort against Llanelli in the Heineken Cup. I came away with the award for Player of the Year, which is a bit of a worry, to be honest; it's been something of a poisoned chalice in recent years. Nigel Redman won it one year and was immediately dropped from the England side, and the same thing had happened to Martin Bayfield and Ben Clarke in the past. I hope it's not a trend that continues.

What was very funny was that the winner's name was supposed to have been a big secret. The RFU insisted that because they would need a photograph of the winner before the announcement was made, then all of the Lions would have to have their photo taken with the trophy before the meal. A nice idea to keep a bit of suspense going for the lads too, you would have thought. The only problem was that someone had forgotten to tape over the engraving which said 'Presented to Martin Johnson', so everyone was holding a trophy that they already knew I'd won! It was farcical!

Still, I was quite surprised to win the trophy because I didn't think I'd had a particularly outstanding season. It was a big honour to be voted for by the journalists and members of the RFU who make up the panel, but I would also like to see an award based on the players voting for their man of the season, although I don't know whether anyone will get it together to organise that in the near future. I gave the trophy to my agent for safekeeping – I didn't think lugging a huge trophy around

South Africa for the entire tour was too clever an idea – and then made my excuses and left for Oatlands.

Friday morning's training session turned out to be quite a laugh. We were doing some line-out work, nothing too strenuous, but Jim Telfer was having a nightmare with everybody's names. Mark Regan was Martin Regan, Scott Quinnell was Derek Quinnell, his dad's name, and Jim couldn't seem to get it right at all, much to our amusement. I thought it was good that people were training with a smile on their faces, because there would doubtless be days when there wouldn't be any laughs at all.

The afternoon's Impact session concentrated on the core values of the tour. Everyone was given a laminate with the tour's rules, 'The Lions Laws', as they were called, which were the things that everyone should think about. The words which were printed on the yellow card were:

Winners, Highest Standards, Discipline (Self and Team), Desire, Dedication, Belief (Self and Others), Identity, Cohesive, Supportive, Openness, Honesty, Enjoyment, Positive, Constructive, Trust, United, Committed, Flexible, Respect Personal Space, Punctual, No Cliques.

The whole point of the week together had been to help us gel as a unit and set standards of behaviour that would allow the squad to perform to the best of its abilities. It wasn't supposed to be authoritarian, laying down tons of rules and regulations, but it was good for everyone that the expectations of the individuals and the group were confirmed like this. I was delighted with the way the players responded, and a bit surprised, too; I'd expected more cynicism. This core values session turned out to be particularly long, but everyone was keen to work at it and put their all into it. We were split into groups to go off and put together a plan for a certain element of the tour. I was in a group with Jerry Guscott, Jim Telfer, Jason Leonard and Barry Williams, and we had to work out how the Disciplinary Committee would work. It was decided that Fran, Geech, Rob Wainwright and I would sit on it and that we would have ultimate power to punish people, with no right of appeal. I wasn't sure that the lads appreciated how much power we were being given, but they seemed happy enough.

I thought that the week had been very successful, almost a dry run of actually being away on tour, and the squad had come together very well. People were chatting together a lot more and were getting to know people they hadn't known before, especially the strangers they were rooming with. I was more than happy to room with someone myself, but the tradition on Lions tours is that the captain gets his own room, and Stan Bagshaw, who was in charge of the rooming arrangements, seemed so put out when I told him I wouldn't mind doubling up that I didn't bother saying anything more and just let him get on with it. I don't think we could have hoped for any more from our time together at Oatlands, and I think we deserved our night on the beers at the end of the week.

The entire squad of 35 players plus management team headed out on the bus to a pub in Weybridge for a good social. I think the idea started out as just going for a couple of quiet pints, but as is the way with these things, by 11.30 p.m. with a few ales inside us we were well up for heading off to a nightclub in Guildford. We would drop the lads who didn't fancy carrying on back at the hotel and then be on our way. At least, that was the plan. As we came back into the grounds at Oatlands there was a sudden massive crashing sound and the tinkle of breaking glass. A branch from one of the trees came straight through the side of the bus. Incredibly, no one was hurt by this rogue piece of woodland, but it scuppered everyone's plans for more entertainment and we had to be content with a couple more at the hotel bar. It was probably a good thing. If we'd gone, someone would definitely have woken up on the streets of Guildford on Saturday morning!

Saturday morning and no hangover! I was glad I hadn't gone too mad the night before and was in a fit state to go and lift some weights and blow the cobwebs away. I still managed to oversleep and miss the bus, though, and had to find my way down to the gym at Twickenham in my own car. I got caught up in traffic for the Middlesex Sevens too, so the morning proved to be a bit more hassle than I'd anticipated. It was my own fault, though, so I couldn't really complain.

We were due to fly out to South Africa at quarter to ten in the evening, so the players' wives and girlfriends had been invited down for a barbecue lunch and to say goodbye. Kay came down and after I'd packed we had a nice, relaxed afternoon wandering about the hotel's beautiful gardens and chatting. I think everyone was pleased to see their partners and it was a fine way to round off our time at Oatlands.

CHAPTER FOUR

Settling in South Africa

Sorry as we were to leave Oatlands, it still felt good to be on our way at last and I was excited about our prospects as I boarded the plane at Heathrow. Virgin Airlines had sponsored the team and we were all flying Upper Class, so everyone was in good spirits and happy to do the necessary photos with the pilot and stewardesses so that Virgin could get some publicity. It turned out that the pilot was a massive rugby fan and so invited me up to the cockpit once we were in the air to have a look round. I was amazed by the technology that these planes now have, especially the 'fly by wire' system where all the navigation and flight courses are plotted by computer. I was a bit worried by the fact that I couldn't see a joystick, until the captain pointed out a tiny controller, like something from a computer game, that had replaced the more traditional huge sticks that everyone recognises. Incredible.

Of course, I slept most of the way down to Johannesburg, but I woke up in time to go back up to the cockpit. Our pilot had radioed ahead and asked for permission to fly over Ellis Park on the way in, which was a lot of fun, and I stayed up front for the landing. Once we were on the ground the pilot wanted me to wave our tour mascot, the cuddly lion, out of the cockpit window, which was my first run-in with the horrible bloody thing!

I know that the toy lion is a traditional part of British Lions tours, but I can't deny that I absolutely hated it. It was a huge great thing, and to my mind looked particularly poncy. I started to dread hearing the words 'Johnno, get off the plane with the lion', or 'Johnno, get off the bus with the lion'. 'How about "Sod off with the lion"?' is what I really wanted to say, and get off the plane last carrying nothing but my CD player, but that wasn't the way things worked out. I was captain and there were certain responsibilities that I had to accept – even if one of them was carrying the bloody mascot!

Once inside the airport I realised how big a deal this Lions tour was to everyone in South Africa. There was an enormous reception laid on for us and we ended up having our photo taken with seemingly thousands of people, including the enormous Springbok and British Lion mascots, two blokes in suits with papier mâché heads, that we'd soon get used to seeing everywhere we went. Fran, Geech and I also met with South Africa's Minister for Sport, Steve Tshwete, who was a very interesting chap and who told us about his own personal association with the Lions. He explained that when the victorious '74 side had been down there he'd been locked up in the notorious Robben Island prison. He told us how, along with all the other political prisoners, he'd listened to all the Test matches on the radio and cheered his heart out each time the Lions won. It was hard to visualise the man who was sitting with us having been locked up so recently, and I couldn't help but think of the enormity of the changes that had taken place in South Africa over the last few years. What kind of a country could have engendered an attitude where so many of the people living there would support a foreign country's sports side against their own? For many black South Africans, the Springboks had represented every-thing that they hated about the apartheid regime, so much so that in 1994 the new government had even tried to change the name of the national team and get rid of the Springboks moniker.

After the press conference we had to take a flight from Jo'burg down to our first base in Durban. By this time everyone was very tired and fractious, and when we arrived at the hotel in Umhlanga, a pleasant suburb of Durban, everyone was happy to have finally arrived at their destination. We were greeted by what would soon become the usual Zulu dancers, but most of the boys were too tired to show more than a polite interest. I think a few of the lads went for a run to get the stiffness out of their legs and try to get acclimatised. Durban is a nice city, and one which I think is still called the Last Outpost of the Empire. It's quite pro-British, so I've always felt pretty much at home there. Of course, any town in South Africa has a certain amount of cultural differences from a British city. If nothing else, then the disparity in wealth between the haves and the have-nots is still fairly shocking. On the one hand you have the exclusive suburb of La Lucia, one of the most beautiful places on earth with some truly gorgeous houses, and then on the other you have people living in what seem like nothing more than the tin shacks you find on allotments back home. Having spent a reasonable amount of time in South Africa it's not as shocking as it once was, but it still makes you think. When I was first down there in 1994 I thought that the whole mood of the country was very optimistic, but I think they're probably now undergoing the first bout of reality. People are realising that things won't change overnight, that the poverty gap will not be shortened in five minutes flat and that there's still a long, long way to go. In some ways, maybe things are getting worse, with more crime and banks even going on strike because there arc so many hold-ups happening. I certainly don't have any answers to the problems, but I do hope that a country that's as beautiful as South Africa can overcome its difficulties.

Our first full day's training on Monday 19 May proved to be a bit of an eye-opener for everyone. I'd forgotten just how hot Durban could be and everyone started the session down at King's Park in lethargic fashion. We'd had a meeting for the forwards the previous night where we'd all agreed that scrummaging would be a key area, possibly *the* key area of play during the tour, and we had decided to put some serious work in right from the off. We had a new scrummaging machine which we soon got to work on, using it to help us get used to the players we hadn't worked with before. Scrummaging is a very technical art and there's no substitute for knowing the players you're working with; their peculiarities, their techniques, their strengths and their weaknesses. We knew that we would have to put some serious work into the scrums to compete with the Springboks, so there could be no slacking.

I was a little concerned that this first day of training was an open session, and it seemed like there were hundreds of press people around. When you're working with the scrum the session is fairly static, which means that you can't run off to another end of the field to work on something else, an old trick that everyone uses to keep the press away. When the press finally manage to lug all their gear down to the end where you've moved to, you simply run back up to the other end. This isn't just done out of spite, though. You can't run through the drills properly in an open session because you don't know who's in that press group. You can bet your bottom dollar that there will be a spy from the opposition's camp in every press corps trying to find out what your strengths and weaknesses are, ready to report back with any useful information they've gleaned. It's even worse when you have cameras filming when you're working on line-out drills. If the calls are caught on tape, then anyone watching can work out where the ball's going to be thrown. Trying to keep one step ahead of the press guys meant that the session didn't run particularly smoothly, and I was glad when we finally packed up for the day.

Graham Rowntree and I went for some lunch at the local shopping mall and, judging by the amount of Springbok merchandising and magazines on the shelves, we soon realised that this tour really was a big deal down here. The South Africans still can't quite get the '74 Lions tour, where the team went home unbeaten, out of their minds. I think it's always an extra spur to the Springboks whenever the Lions go there not to suffer the same humiliation, but it puts extra pressure on the Lions party too, because the South Africans are so fired up for these Tests in particular. I knew that we'd have to match them every step of the way for passion, and for fitness, if we were to stand a chance. To that end, the management had done a deal with a chain of gyms across South Africa so that we would be able to use any of their facilities, so in the afternoon I made use of the arrangement and went for a workout. I have to say, the amount of good-looking women in the place made me pretty sure there wouldn't be any shortage of volunteers for gym sessions during the tour!

The evening's team meeting proved to be a lively affair, with everyone deciding on who should be in charge of the players' court. For those who don't know about the form on rugby tours, the court is set up by the players and is the place where people can be called to answer all kinds of ludicrous and often trumped-up charges. Fines are payable, but the real reason behind the court is simply for everyone to have a good laugh together. Keith Wood was chosen as judge (he must have the necessary look of authority), while Ieuan Evans became clerk of the court, Mark 'Ronnie' Regan defence lawyer, Rob Wainwright prosecution, and Tim Stimpson finemaster. David Young, Simon Shaw and Tom Smith were nominated as henchmen, for obvious reasons. I wouldn't imagine that anyone would be too keen to get those guys on their back over unpaid fines.

On a more serious note, the players' representatives were also nominated. These are the people who are consulted if there are any serious problems with the management that the players feel need addressing. It's quite an important role if things aren't going so well on a tour, less so if things are running smoothly, so I hoped they wouldn't find themselves too busy during the next seven weeks. The players chosen were Scott Gibbs, Paul Wallace, Alan Tait and Lawrence Dallaglio, and I felt they offered a good blend and had a sound attitude.

We ended the evening with a 45-minute line-out meeting. I was 'all meetinged out' by this stage, so I probably wasn't in the best frame of mind for making a useful contribution. I was keen to get David Young involved at this stage. He was very experienced and I thought his knowledge would prove useful. I was quietly confident about our prospects in the line-out, though. Both Rob Wainwright and Eric Miller are good jumpers and I thought they would give us options; we wouldn't simply be throwing the ball to the same guy all the time. Ronnie Regan wasn't involved in the meeting and wasn't particularly happy about it. I think he was a bit paranoid, but when I told him not to worry as he was going to be involved in defensive work he seemed happy enough. At this stage of the tour it seemed fairly likely that he would win a Test spot because his throwing at line-outs was considered to be better than Keith Wood's, our other hooker who was competing for the Test place. And both players had a lot more experience than Barry Williams. Whatever the politics of hookers, though, I was happy when the line-out session finally broke up and I could get off.

I pondered the first selection meeting of the tour that was going to take place the following evening. My groin was giving me a little bit of grief and the management had mentioned to me today that it might be better if I didn't play in the first game against Eastern Province. While I knew that it might make good sense to rest up for a while longer, the fact that it was traditional for the captain to lead the Lions out in the first game of the tour made me think it would be a bit of a weird decision not to pick me. I wondered how I'd feel if I wasn't going to lead the team on to the field, but decided that it really wasn't worth worrying about and that I should simply concentrate on getting myself fully fit as quickly as possible. I'd imagined that Jim, Fran and Geech had a pretty set idea in their minds as to who would be playing in the first three games anyway, so there was no point in me worrying about things too much.

I had a quick chat with the TV crew who'd been with us since Oatlands and thought that they were nice enough blokes, but I didn't fancy the idea of having them filming in team meetings. There are certain things that get said in those meetings which should always stay between four walls, things that you definitely wouldn't like to be broadcast to the nation. I'd have to wait and see how things worked out the next day and decide whether or not to make a fuss about it.

The itinerary for Tuesday included a double training session, so the boys decided they'd have a pint or two in a local bar on Monday night, purely so that they could spend some time away from the hotel. You have to be careful if you get into a routine of simply training then going back to the hotel, because you could end up spending your entire tour doing exactly the same things all the time. Unfortunately, I was due in a selection meeting for the first game so I wasn't able to get out. That's just the way it goes sometimes. I'd damaged my AC joint, just by my left shoulder, during training, and this was an extra headache for me. In a way, though, it made things a little easier, as it was another good reason to have a rest until Cape Town, to get myself into as good a shape as possible. The cameras did end up in the selection meeting, although they proved not to be as distracting as I'd thought they might be and the meeting went well.

It was decided that Jason Leonard would captain the side in Port Elizabeth ahead of Tim Rodber and Lawrence Dallaglio for the main reason that he had more Tests under his belt and greater all-round experience. I thought that the press would most likely be focusing on myself and Tim for the game; on me because I wasn't playing and on Tim because he'd been sent off the last time he'd played in Port Elizabeth, for England in 1994. I wasn't worried about Tim's ability to handle the extra pressure, though. He's been around a long time and has a very level-headed attitude. Overall I was happy with the team selection, although I felt we still had a lot of work to do on our organisation. There was no way that we'd gelled together as yet – how could we? – but I was confident that this would come with time. I knew the game would be tough as this was actually an Eastern Province Invitation XV, which meant that they'd drafted in some stronger players, but I hoped we'd be able to get off to a winning start.

Once the selection meeting broke up I decided to sit in on a get-together for all the backs. It was my third night in South Africa and I was in what felt like my hundredth meeting. I remembered a bit of advice that I'd been given by both Tim Rodber and Phil de Glanville, that I should make sure I took time for myself. They'd both warned me that as captain you could soon find yourself spending so much time dealing with other people's problems that it would be almost impossible to get yourself properly prepared, which would be stupid. I recognised that so far I hadn't been able to do that and promised myself some more quality time soon.

Still, I wasn't really complaining. Everyone was trying their best to make us feel welcome. Scottish Provident had given us a boogie box for the team coach, which I knew would improve the journeys, and the South African rugby union had provided me with a mobile phone, which would also come in handy.

The team was announced on the Wednesday morning after we had all had a good night's sleep, and everyone seemed reasonably content with the decisions that had been made. My Leicester team-mate Will Greenwood was selected, which I was pleased about seeing as he hadn't even got an England cap. The pack seemed solid with Jason and Lawrence Dallaglio in there and Neil Jenkins was given a chance to stake an early Test claim at full-back. It would be interesting to see from the stands how the side performed.

We dedicated the morning to a two-and-a-half-hour training session under a burning Durban sun, which was hard going, but the boys all worked manfully at their game. There certainly seemed to be no question of a problem with anyone's attitude. I wasn't really able to take a full part in training because my AC joint was really giving me gyp, so I had to content myself with some 150-metre sprints to keep my fitness level up. A few of the other boys also took knocks and had to come off, which I suppose was to be expected. I felt that injuries would play a vital role in how the tour unfolded. If we could ride our luck a little bit and steer clear of too many problems, it would make the task in hand so much easier for us.

When we got back to the hotel I had to go into a pre-game press conference. Jason got plenty of interest after being chosen as captain and I wasn't particularly envious of him having to answer so many inane questions. I had to do numerous one-to-one interviews myself and tried hard to sound enthusiastic, but secretly I was dreading the thought of an entire tour having to deal with this kind of stuff. One particular Afrikaner reporter was very frustrating, reading out questions from a printed sheet of paper that seemed to go on forever and which he delivered with all the enthusiasm of a man who had never seen a rugby game in his life and who frankly didn't care to either. Patience, they say, is a virtue and, boy, was I starting to learn that! It was a good job that we had the afternoon free after such teeth-pulling torture!

In the event it actually turned out to be a very interesting afternoon. Someone had organised a trip down to the beach to meet up with the Shark Board, a government organisation that has been set up to control the shark population in the Durban area. The guys who ran it were pleased to see us and taught us a lot about their work. The best bit as far as I was concerned was when they dissected a fairly small shark for us. There were all kinds of weird things in there, including whole fish inside the shark's belly, which was strange to see, but very interesting all the same. Then we were shown a film about sharks, which most of us were expecting – maybe hoping – to be a bit gruesome. In fact it turned out to be pretty tame, but we all had to hide our disappointment and pretend that it was all very interesting stuff.

Once they'd got over their shark film frustration, a few of the boys remarked during the rest of the Shark Board trip that they were a little surprised I wasn't playing in the opening game. They didn't seem overly concerned about it when I brushed it off saying I was being rested after my long domestic season and that it wasn't that big a deal.

Back at the hotel I decided that I fancied going out to eat. The food in the hotel was getting a bit bland and I don't particularly like fish so I wasn't exactly what you'd call spoilt for choice. Doddie Weir fancied a change too, so we went around the corner to a local restaurant to get ourselves a good dose of saturated fats. Doddie's a nice bloke, very chatty and the life and soul of things, so he's always good company. Mind you, I think I would have gone out to eat with anyone by that stage, just to see some real life instead of the inside of a hotel. The talk was pleasant and, as is the way of things, always seemed to get back to rugby-related matters. I suppose that's only natural when you all have roughly the same field of experience.

We talked a little about the pay structure for the tour for some reason. It seemed to me that things were organised very simply and fairly too. Everyone was paid the same fee for the tour and there would also be a bonus for winning the series. It can be argued that the players who won Test caps should have been paid more than the players who didn't, but I think such a system could have been potentially divisive, whereas it was vital in the early stages of the tour to build team spirit. It's possible that the next time the Lions tour, with professionalism much more embedded in the foundations of the game, there will be a system where, say, the people who have more Lions caps already will get more money. I'd say that's almost inevitable. The Lions is a unique situation where the players only come together once every four years, so things might not be so easy to structure as it would be for players' regular international sides. I'd be lying if I said that I hadn't looked at the way the pay is structured in the England set-up and thought that certain players hadn't done as much in the game as others and yet were still on the same money. But there's a way of quantifying performance for England. You can see how long someone has been involved at the highest level and how many caps they've won. It's much more difficult with the Lions. Everyone has already proved themselves to a certain degree. Whatever the eventual outcome, though, Doddie and I had an interesting conversation and it was a good way to round off another day.

Thursday morning proved to be frustrating for me again. I couldn't take part in any of the contact sessions because my shoulder was still troubling me. The boys had a hard, two-hour session and there I was, feeling impotent again. I think I felt the separation more acutely than I would have done had I not been captain. If I'd been there simply as a member of the squad, then I could have just thought about what was best for Johnno and then done what was best for Johnno. That's a bit of an 'I'm all right Jack' attitude, I suppose, but that was the truth of it. As captain I felt that I wanted to be out there doing it, that I *should* be out there doing it, leading by example, doing my bit to keep the spirit of the squad going. I didn't like sitting on the sidelines watching people fill in for me, doing my hard work. I felt guilty about missing out, but from a purely rugby point of view I had a suspicion that it wouldn't be doing me much harm. I'd played so many games towards the end of the domestic season that I knew I wasn't short of match practice, which is obviously the best kind of practice you can get.

The injury meant that I had time to sit and watch how the squad was developing. Looking at the session, it was obvious that John

Bentley was becoming a focal point of everything that was going on. Bentos is a real character and for this session had managed to talk the film crew into giving him a little hand-held camera to film stuff on. He was always going up to people and winding them up to try and get them to do something daft on film, which was always fun to watch. The funny thing about that camera is that Bentos eventually claimed that it got stolen. It wasn't beyond the realms of possibility because throughout the tour there was a lot of petty pilfering going on from the players' rooms. I had some money taken along with a mobile phone and some traveller's cheques during the tour, and a lot of the other lads were relieved of this or that. Bentos stuck to his story that it had been pinched, but knowing him . . . well, you wouldn't put anything past him!

I think by this time the lads were really desperate to get the show on the road. We'd been together for two weeks and hadn't played in one competitive match. When you're travelling about and playing games the time flies, but we'd been keeping our powder dry for a long time and I think people were getting a bit tense. No one was really letting the frustration show, but there was a feeling in the air that people wanted to get going, wanted to get on a rugby pitch. I tried to tell the lads to enjoy the moment, the calm before the storm, and take advantage of it; I knew it wouldn't be long before they'd all be crying out for a rest.

The bad news from the session was that Tim Rodber was coming down with a virus and didn't look like he'd make the game. It was a blow, but at least the potential problem of repercussions from his sending-off in Port Elizabeth in '94 was solved: he wasn't fit enough to play and Scott Quinnell was drafted into the side.

We managed to take our minds off this feeling of waiting around for something to happen by having dinner at Langoustines, one of the best seafood restaurants in Durban and a really nice spot. It's always a good idea for the entire touring party to go out to eat together, but when there are 50 people involved it can often turn into a military operation. What invariably happens is that there's an almighty wait after you've ordered your food before it finally arrives, which is understandable considering the number of people the restaurants are catering for, but it can be very frustrating. We managed to while away the waiting time at Langoustines by playing 'Guess who's coming to dinner'. The principle of the game is simple: everyone writes down the name of a person, famous, unknown or even fictional, and all the names are folded up and put into a glass. Then one person will pick a name out of the glass and challenge someone else around the table. For example, I could say to Ieuan Evans, 'Ieuan, is Sly Stallone coming to dinner?' Now if Ieuan had written down Sly Stallone, then he'd have to answer 'Yes, Sly's coming to dinner' and he'd be out of the game. The winner, of course, is the last one to be guessed. It's not brain surgery, but it's a fun way to pass the time and if you know guys well enough you can start to work out who would have written which character down. Neil Back, for example, would always write something crude, so you could spot the name he'd chosen a mile off. The funniest thing was that Mark Regan couldn't get a grip on the rules and asked someone if Steven Segal was coming to dinner, even though his name wasn't even in the pot. With the beers flowing everyone thought this was a particularly hilarious comment! 'Guess who's coming to dinner' passed the time well enough at Langoustines and the food was fantastic when it arrived, so all in all a good night was had by everyone.

We got back to the hotel at a reasonable time and packed ready to leave Umhlanga for Port Elizabeth the following day. It was going to be a long, probably not good, Friday with a journey the day before a game. Not ideal preparation, but, again, that was just something the lads would have to deal with.

We trained on the Friday morning in Durban, a split session with the next day's team leaving early. For the lads who were likely to be playing the following Wednesday this would be a hard session, the equivalent to a normal Monday workout during the season, while the following day's team did a light workout, then left in a separate bus. The lads who weren't playing did some speed tests, 15- and 30-metre sprint work. Ieuan was looking particularly quick during these exercises, and Tony Underwood was proving himself no slouch either. It was good to see the lads looking sharp and up for it.

There was a lot of work done on rucking, too, with Jim Telfer taking charge. He wasn't perhaps as rabid as we thought he might have been by this stage. Everyone had been a little wary of Jim from the off. He's so enthusiastic about the game and the training that there's a danger that certain types of players will switch off from his screaming. The English lads are probably a little bit, well, cocky, and might have taken against Jim's rabble-rousing style. Emotional team talks have to be delivered by the right person, at the right time, otherwise a lot of players will just think 'bollocks'. To Jim's credit, his style was very effective and the players respected him greatly. Jim likes to shout at people, give them a clip round the ear and all the rest of it, but everyone responded well. He transferred his enthusiasm to everyone else when I thought he might have some problems, so all credit to him. Mind you, it was quite funny, too. When Jim got everyone practising tackling by hitting the pads, he said everyone should scream when they attacked them. As you might expect, some of the boys were letting out the most ridiculous cries, really taking the piss. I think Rob Wainwright was particularly outstanding in that department, which gave everyone a good laugh. But at the end of the day everything was taken in the right spirit, and despite the hard work we all had a good time.

We were due to leave the hotel at four in the afternoon for the flight to Port Elizabeth, so I had a leisurely lunch with Jerry Guscott, Ieuan and Dai Young. I found that it was useful to have a chat with Jerry. He's been around at the highest level for a long time and has some very sound ideas behind that carefree appearance. A lot of people have the impression that he's a bit lackadaisical, maybe even a touch arrogant, but I think it's more a question of Jerry not being afraid to show his confidence in his own abilities and opinions. If you think about it, Jerry's just being truthful about the way he feels about things. Maybe he annoys some people, but he's such a good player that you can't ignore him. Or his opinions. And I didn't.

CHAPTER FIVE

A Match at Last

The flight down to Port Elizabeth was uneventful. I think most of the players were starting to really turn their attentions to the next day's game against Eastern Province. Everyone knew that it was important to get off to a good start. I felt it wouldn't have been the end of the world if we'd lost the first game, but psychologically it would put us in a great frame of mind if we came out of the match with a victory under our belts. There are different schools of thought as to how people approach the provincial matches on a tour. The All Blacks, for example, can't countenance the idea of losing a single match, whereas the French use all the provincial games as a build-up to the Test matches and don't seem particularly concerned if they lose them. I would say that my attitude was somewhere in the middle. I wanted to get off to a winning start, but I thought we could lose quite a few of the provincial games and it wouldn't have made much difference to the overall strategy of winning the series. Most good players take the stance that there's nothing more important than the next game, but if we'd lost to Eastern Province I would have been able to deal with it.

When we touched down, the airport was full of local dancers greeting us, something we were getting quite used to by now. I don't think anyone was really in the mood, but we all tried to look appreciative. When we arrived at the hotel about half-past seven there was no denying that the place was a bit of a downer. It was very ordinary-looking and we didn't have a dining area that was separate from the rest of the guests. We were just tucked away in a little corner which made the lads feel like they were in a goldfish bowl every time they went to eat. The hotel didn't really have a very good feel to it and that bothered me. I like all my preparations to be spot on and, although I wasn't even playing in the game, I felt a bit uneasy about where we were.

There were other problems too. Some of the luggage and all of our medical kit was delayed coming in from Durban, which really got Fran's goat. At the team meeting that night he went on about how the food had been crap at dinner (it had, actually) and how the South Africans were pissing us around with the delays to our gear. He ordered a load of sandwiches there and then and got them brought to the team room so that the players could at least have something edible. I thought that was a good move and typical of the way Fran was running things. If something needed doing he just went ahead and did it. If something hadn't been budgeted for yet was needed, it didn't matter; Fran just went ahead and got it anyway. The little things that he did were really appreciated by the players, because they knew that he was in touch with what they were thinking, feeling and needing. Fran asked a rhetorical question too: 'Are we going to let them get to us with this kind of crap?' I don't think he really needed any reply. He knew what we were all thinking.

Saturday, the first game day of the tour. At last. I woke up feeling a bit nervous, hoping that things would get off to a winning start, but soon had the opportunity to take my mind off things when I joined up with the rest of the non-players and left the hotel for fitness testing up at the local university with Lions fitness adviser Dave McLean. It was pretty hard work, as it turned out, having to do a lot of ten- and 15-second bursts of sprinting and running all over the field. I have a pretty good endurance fitness level for this kind of thing so I didn't suffer particularly badly, but most of the forwards hate this stuff and decided to let their feelings on the subject be known. I was impressed with the way Dave handled this minor rebellion. People were going on about how this wasn't going to benefit them, blah, blah, blah, but Dave pointed out that we'd all talked many times about accepting the challenges of the tour and now people were already backing away from the very first challenge on the training pitch. Once they'd had a flea in their ear everyone got down to work and, as is the way with these things, it then turned out to be a really enjoyable session.

Following our workout we all got straight on the bus to head out to the Adcock Stadium in Port Elizabeth to coach kids from the townships. I always have very mixed feelings about this kind of stuff. While the enthusiasm of the kids is immense, I can't help but wonder what the real point of these events is. I can't see that me coaching for half an hour and having some pictures taken is going to benefit these kids at all. I go there, I put the right T-shirt and cap on and stand around and smile for the cameras, something which seems of a lot more benefit to the sponsors than it is to the kids. Maybe I'm too cynical about the whole thing and I'm underestimating the impact of a team like the Lions simply turning up. After all, when we were giving out badges and baseball caps at Adcock Stadium, the kids were going absolutely ballistic trying to grab one. Maybe that's the real benefit of doing these sessions. Whatever the politics, though, it was great to see such naturally gifted players having a go. The ball-handling skills that some of the lads displayed was fantastic, and they were all training barefoot, without any of the proper equipment. There are kids in Britain who are much older than these boys and who have been playing rugby for years who aren't as good as them, which I suppose should make us all worry for the future. Natural aptitude can be a frightening thing.

After returning to the hotel from the coaching session, I had to get myself prepared for the match. It's always a little bit strange for me going to a game that I'm not playing in. It's difficult to be simply hanging around the place. Where do you go? What do you do? In many ways it makes me feel a lot more tense than if I'm actually playing in the match myself. You want the team to win, but there's nothing that you can do about it. I generally try to keep out of the way a little bit, so I said good luck to the lads and quickly took my seat in the stand. The Telkom Stadium, once known as Boet Erasmus Stadium, is a large, open ground and the weather was very hot, which immediately made me wonder how the lads would cope with their first competitive game in this heat. As the game kicked off I felt really tense. It's hellish. The exhilaration when the team does something right is greater watching from the stands than even being on the field, but the tension when the side is under pressure is almost unbearable. The truth is that I don't find watching matches particularly enjoyable because I'm too emotionally involved.

The game itself started well for us. I thought we played some really good stuff in the opening 20 minutes: we were moving the ball around well and Jerry ran in a nice try to get us settled down. The problem was that we started trying to force the play too much and a lot of passes started to go astray. I could see from the stands how the heat was starting to sap everybody's strength and it was really noticeable that the energy level had dropped. We needed to hold on to the ball better, but we allowed Eastern Province back into the game and let them put more and more pressure on us. Our defence was doing quite well, but we still lost our way and went 11–10 behind early in the second half, and I started to get worried. You could see the South Africans' tails were up and the crowd got excited. I wondered whether we might well suffer our first defeat in the opening game, but the boys rallied well and came back strongly to run in another four tries – another one from Jerry and one each from Will Greenwood, Doddie and Tony Underwood. Neil Jenkins was his usual reliable self, kicking two penalties and slotting home four conversions, which made me think it would be difficult for any kicker, even a good one like Tim Stimpson, to dislodge him from a Test side. In the end we ran out comfortable 39–11 winners, but at one stage things weren't looking anywhere near as rosy.

The positive thing from this opening fixture was that there were more good points than bad that came out of the match. Scott Quinnell, Lawrence Dallaglio, Will and Jerry were my pick of the side, although Tom Smith and Keith Wood also did very well. Rob Howley had looked sharp and the important thing was that the side had shown the ambition to play stylish rugby. We certainly could have played a tighter game, but don't forget this was a brand new team so no one really had the right to be overly critical. And, best of all, Scott Quinnell had put the huge Springbok lock Kobus Wiese flat on his arse with a crunching tackle, which I thought was a huge psychological blow for the Springboks. Some of the boys felt a bit deflated in the dressing-room after the game, but I told them they shouldn't be down about the performance and that there was plenty of time to improve on the weaker aspects of the play, like the line-out, which hadn't really functioned too well.

We went for a bit of a chat with the Eastern Province players after the game and had a really pleasant time. I ended up talking with Hannes Marais, who'd captained the Springboks against Fran's Lions team in 1974. He seemed a nice enough bloke and we spent some time discussing Eastern Province rugby and the general state of the game. I think some of the lads who'd been playing were looking to get away because the heat had really sapped their strength, so we soon made our excuses and drifted back to the hotel.

The idea that we had to engender team spirit by going out to eat as a squad once a week saw us heading out to a local restaurant *en masse*. To be honest, this turned out to be a very bad move. The restaurant had had the clever idea of putting up a sign saying 'The Lions Are Coming' or something, so the place was packed with people gawping at us – and, of course, we had to wait two hours for our food. It was a pretty annoying way to end a relatively successful day, and I decided to make sure we found more private places to eat in future. This is, of course, easier said than done. Rugby is perceived completely differently in South Africa from the way it is back home. It's a major sport, so the level of interest in a touring rugby side is far greater over there than it ever would be in Britain or Ireland. Trying to find somewhere where we wouldn't be bothered wasn't going to be easy.

CHAPTER SIX

Border

After a brief but good training session for the non-players on the Sunday morning and light recovery work for those who'd been involved in the game, we were due to leave Port Elizabeth for East London, where we would set up base for four nights for the game against Border. My AC was feeling a lot better even after working out, so that made me more cheery as we headed to the airport. After we arrived in East London, however, my mood was soon blackened by a group of drum majorettes meeting us with all the usual hoo-ha. I suppose it made a change from traditional dancers, but I would have preferred something a lot more low-key any day.

If low-key was what I wanted, then I soon got it when the bus that was taking us from the airport to the Holiday Inn suffered a broken accelerator cable and we ended up crawling along the road at a princely ten miles an hour. Eventually the bus completely packed up, and we had to wait patiently for about an hour before another one came to pick us up. We waited in almost total silence; everyone was so tired that they weren't in the mood for any kind of wisecracks, even in such bizarre circumstances.

I don't think I've ever been so glad to see a hotel room as I was that day. For the first time on the tour I ended up sharing a room. Simon Shaw's grandfather had been ill and had sadly died, so Simon obviously needed some privacy to make personal phone calls and what have you. Doddie moved out of Simon's room and in with me. I must admit I was quite happy to have another person around. It's easy to get used to having your own room, but I think living with your team-mates is part of the touring experience.

The selection meeting for Wednesday's game took place on the Sunday night as usual and again it was decided that I wouldn't play. Most of the players from the first match were to be rested and I wasn't bothered about the decision that I wouldn't get a game, but I knew that I'd probably have to face a barrage of questions, not only from the press but also from my own team-mates as to why I'd been chosen as captain and yet hadn't even been on the field of play yet. We'd tried to keep my injury worries away from the press and had been pretty successful so far, and I knew that Fran would be very good at toeing the party line for the media, putting out the story about needing me to rest and about how we were gearing all our preparations for the first Test. I thought that would be enough to keep people off our backs – at least for a while – and went to sleep relatively contented.

I woke up the following morning to a very wet and windy East London, which was a bit of a culture shock after all the glorious weather and stifling heat that we'd been getting used to. I don't know if the foul weather contributed to some of the foul moods during morning training, but it wasn't a happy camp and there was a bit of a dust-up between Mark Regan and Barry Williams. I don't even know what started it, but things can and do happen in the heat of the moment when everyone's really going at it hammer and tongs. I thought it was pretty standard stuff and people pulled them apart quickly enough to calm things down before things had really got out of hand. I wasn't unduly worried about a bit of fisticuffs. I had a bit of a chat with the management about the incident and then got things sorted out between the two of them, and as far as I'm aware there was no hangover from the incident throughout the rest of the tour. Both lads seemed to just get on with things after that, so everything was smoothed over easily enough.

It was a particularly tough training session for the Wednesday team and they seemed pretty wound up and tense overall, which I didn't think was particularly healthy. The problem I had was that Rob Wainwright was captain for the game against Border and Jason Leonard was running the other team in training, so there was no place for me to slot in seamlessly. It was the first time in what felt like ages that I'd been able to participate fully, but I was sort of stuck in the middle and ended up running with Rob's team, which was probably a little bit awkward for both of us. Still, a lot of people were getting involved in teamwork together for the first time, so it probably wasn't just me who was feeling out of place. I for one was glad when it was finally over – the session hadn't been too much fun – and we could get back to the hotel and out of the rain.

The afternoon was taken up with a workout in the gym and two video sessions, where we looked back at the Eastern Province game to see what we could learn from the performance. Watching the match again it was obvious that we needed to improve our performance in the line-out and that our tackling would have to be better for the rest of the tour. Identifying such bad parts of play is the whole point of having the video sessions; it wouldn't do much good if we just looked at the good points of our own performance – that way we'd never improve – and I felt it was a useful session. I also organised a senior players' meeting for myself, Jason Leonard, Lol Dallaglio, Rob Wainwright and Ieuan Evans to go through any issues that people felt like raising and to check that the mood of the players was generally happy and that there weren't any problems which needed addressing. I was pleased to get reports that everyone was in a positive frame of mind and that there didn't seem to be any problems, there were no cliques forming or the like. Touch wood, things seemed to be running very smoothly from the players' perspective.

In the evening most of the guys decided they'd take up an oppor-tunity to go go-karting, which sounded like a good idea. Unfortunately, duty called and I had to meet with Fran to discuss some of the more peripheral issues around the tour. One of those issues involved discussing how Sky television's access to players for interviews would work. We felt that the TV company should be prepared to put some money into the players' kitty for the interviews we were giving them. Certainly, they'd bought the rights to the games, but we didn't see why they should get extra privileges just because of that. I thought they should at least show willing and put some kind of fee in, and Fran agreed to go and talk to them.

There were also other points to be dealt with, like making sure tickets for players' guests were organised well in advance so that they wouldn't have any distractions just before big matches. Girlfriends were also discussed and a few ground rules were emphasised. It was decided that it wouldn't be conducive to a good atmosphere on the tour to have girlfriends staying around the hotel, which I thought was fair enough.

Fran had no problem with people having their girlfriends, wives, whatever, visiting, and there was no need to be rigid with the rules, but if a player wanted to be with their partner, then they would have to go to see them in another hotel away from the touring party. Most of the players' partners, it has to be said, were very good about the rules, because they understand exactly what's involved in being on a rugby tour, so as far as I was aware there weren't any problems at all. The whole point of all these little issues being addressed now was that hopefully they could be sorted out and there wouldn't be any distractions about by the time the first Test came around.

I still wasn't involved with the team for the following day's game against Border during the Tuesday-morning training session, of course, but after discussions with Fran I now knew that I'd be making my first appearance on the coming Saturday in the match in Cape Town against Western Province. I knew that I would be ready for that game, but the truth was that I had to be ready for it come what may. If I'd missed a third match in a row I don't think the press would have worn any more excuses and all hell would have broken loose. As it was, I felt pretty good fitness-wise, and safe in the knowledge that I'd make my tour début on Saturday it was a little bit easier not being involved in the thick of the action for the Border game. I'd also been told that Newlands was sold out for the Western Province match, which made me want the game to come around even quicker. It's always a buzz to play in a big stadium in front of a full house. It's one of the most exciting feelings in the world and just the thought of experiencing it soon gave me a real buzz – even helping me deal with the weather in East London, which yet again was very wet indeed. I also got the news that Tim Rodber would again be out for the next day's game after cutting his head open in training. The injury needed stitches, and although Tim had only been selected to sit on the bench for the game, he was still very pissed off to be forced to miss out on being a part of the action yet again. It didn't seem like he was having much luck on tour so far.

I managed to spend the afternoon having a turn on the go-karts which the lads had been messing about with the night before while I'd been meeting with Fran. I went along with some of the guys from the film crew and we had a good laugh. Duncan the cameraman managed to come out on top, so I'd be very surprised if there isn't a huge amount of footage of him receiving his trophy when the film finally gets made! Go-karting, however, wasn't the highlight of the day for me. That came when the security guys who'd been guarding us offered me a lift back to the hotel in their armoured personnel carrier. Until we'd arrived in East London I'd been quite surprised that we hadn't been assigned any security people to keep an eye on us. On the occasions that I'd been in South Africa previously there had always been someone around to look out for us, protect us if necessary, but it was only when we got to East London that anyone was assigned to us. Whatever, the guys must have been bored out of their minds watching us go-karting and thought they'd liven things up by having a 'civvy' on board their vehicle. In one fell swoop I'd gone from having no security whatsoever to being in charge of four pump-action shotguns, roaming the streets of East London. I looked out of the portholes as we cruised back to the hotel and thought how weird it all was. You'd never see a sight like this on the streets of Leicester, that was for sure! It was definitely a thrill to be on board, and I must admit I felt like a kid and really enjoyed the whole experience.

The evening didn't quite match up to that particular thrill, though. There was a Border players' meeting at 6 p.m. which I went to even though I wasn't part of the side, and then I mooched around the hotel, not doing very much at all. I was just killing time before the next day's game.

And what a strange affair the Border game turned out to be. It was really hard yakka for the lads if nothing else. The pitch was pretty much waterlogged (ironic for a part of the country that called itself 'the heart of the Sunshine Coast') and we very nearly came unstuck. From my vantage point in the stand I felt we tried to play far too much rugby given the appalling conditions. The team was so keen to show that we could play a running game as well as any team in the Southern Hemisphere that we were trying to chuck the ball around and get a lot of movement when it was simply impossible to do so. On a day like that, the best policy you can adopt is to hit the opposition early, rack up points on the board as quickly as you can to put them out of touch as soon as possible and then try the fancy stuff. You shouldn't try to force things too much, and simply keep hold of the ball and kick your penalties when you get them. John Bentley put us ahead with a try after two or three minutes and we really should have taken the game by the ocruff of the neck then, but we made mistakes like we had done in the Eastern Province game and let Border back into the match.

I was so nervous throughout the second half that it was almost painful, and when there were just seven minutes to go and we were four points behind I thought I was going to explode. We showed a lot of guts to rectify the situation and come through at the end with a try from Rob Wainwright and a penalty put over by Tim Stimpson, but we shouldn't have made such hard work of a team that was only rated 11th in South Africa. An 18–14 win is an 18–14 win at the end of the day, but I think everyone knew that we'd have to put in a much better performance than that if we were going to compete with the best club sides in South Africa, never mind the Springboks themselves. Overall, splashing around in the rain at Border proved to be a big disappointment.

The match was particularly tough on Paul Grayson. He hadn't played a competitive match for three months and the conditions were particularly difficult, but he missed five kicks at goal and really didn't look anywhere near match fit. I think it had been in the back of his mind that he wasn't fully fit since we had first met up for the tour in England, but he must have been holding on to the hope that rest and the fine weather in South Africa might aid his recovery. It's something that you do as a sportsman. You cling on to any hope you can that things might come good for you. Rest, extra training. whatever. You'll try anything. I've lost count of the number of times I've been virtually crippled on a Thursday and then, come Saturday and the match, the adrenaline kicks in and that gets me through the game. I was worried about the effect Grays's fitness problem would have on team selection during the rest of the tour too. Tim Stimpson was the best full-back we had at this particular point, but he wasn't a noted goal-kicker. With Grays out of the reckoning, that would mean there was only one kicker of real note in the entire squad, Neil Jenkins. And there were other injury worries too. Scott Gibbs had hobbled out of the Border game early in the second half with suspected damaged ankle ligaments that we thought might be pretty serious, and Tom Smith was still suffering with a stiff neck that he'd picked up against Eastern Province. It really didn't seem like we were having any luck, and I had to grasp the crumbs of comfort that Alan Tait and John Bentley had both played particularly well for us. The whole aim of the Border game as far as I was concerned was to get in and get out with a win in our pockets and no injuries, but we hadn't quite managed it. And, on the whole, the match really hadn't been anything to write home about.

The last thing I wanted to do after a game like that was attend the post-match reception, especially when I had to sit through some below-average jokes being cracked by the Border manager. Of course, I know you have to turn up to these things out of respect for your hosts, but it wasn't the easiest task I'd had to take care of as captain. I looked on the bright side and thought how difficult things would have been if we'd lost the match – and then got on with the grip and grin.

We returned to the hotel in a bit of a sombre mood and had dinner at a local seafood restaurant where, to be honest, the mood didn't really pick up all that much. A wet Wednesday night in East London having just scraped through a match can't really be anyone's idea of a good time, so everyone took themselves off to bed, thinking how things always look better in the morning.

CHAPTER SEVEN

Leading the Lions Out

Things obviously *do* always look better in the morning. The good news at the beginning of 29 May was that Gibbsy's ankle trouble wasn't anywhere near as bad as had first been thought, which pleased me no end. Gibbsy was such a vital member of the squad that it was hard to overestimate his value to us. His sheer physical presence on the pitch was colossal and he was one of the players who brought a lot to the squad, as he was used to an ultra-professional attitude having played in rugby league. The way that Gibbsy, Allan Bateman and John Bentley conducted themselves off the pitch and on the training field was inspirational to all of us, and if Scott wasn't the loudest bloke on tour, then he was a prime example of someone who leads by his actions. He had a very physical edge in games and training, which was what we all needed to be able to compete with well-drilled and teak-tough South African teams.

Of course, where the league players have been concerned, there have always been mutterings and murmurings about the use of steroids. When players have left the game of union for league they've often filled out and bulked up considerably. I'll state here and now, though, that it's very easy for people who want to snipe to talk about steroids, when maybe they should just be asking whether these guys have put the work in to improve their physiques. When you see the effort they've put in and know that they've done it full time for a number of years, then to my mind it doesn't seem that bizarre that you will see the results. The rugby league clubs know about the physical presence that's required in their game and can help players to bulk up, but if you look at Allan Bateman he doesn't seem particularly different in build from when he first left rugby union. Scott Gibbs certainly does, but I for one don't believe that Scott Gibbs is on any kind of chemical at all. He's not what you'd call freakishly big. To my mind, he knew he had to get bigger, he worked hard and now he's reaping the rewards. And he made himself an even better rugby player.

Even without having Gibbsy at the morning's training session, however, it was a particularly good session. I felt very comfortable with the forwards who'd been selected to play alongside me in my first match, because six of them were English and I obviously knew their styles of play and little nuances almost inside out. I think it was a good idea to select a pack of players who knew each other well for this vital fixture. We'd not done too well against Border and the Eastern Province match was only satisfactory, so questions were starting to be asked of our scrummaging abilities. To start with a forward line-up of Rowntree, Williams, Leonard, Dallaglio, Shaw, Hill, Rodber and myself made sense to me. There was no fixed idea in the selectors' minds as to what the permutation for the Test match would be – everything was still up for grabs – but we thought that at the very least that group of players would give us a solid base to set up a win against Western Province. Already it was becoming apparent that there was so much competition for places that it wouldn't be possible to decide on a definitive team for the first Test until just before the game itself, so that everyone would have an equal chance to make the side. There weren't too many players who were head and shoulders above their rivals for Test places and that was exactly what we wanted: healthy competition for places right across the pitch.

I think everyone was glad to be out of the rainy and low-key atmosphere around East London and to be moving on and heading down to Cape Town. The flight was on a little 45-seater and there were some great views to be seen out of the windows almost as soon as we took off, but I couldn't keep my eyes open and drifted off to sleep almost immediately. I was getting particularly good at nodding off at a moment's notice but, in my defence, I had been training pretty heavily all week and I think it had taken a lot out of me. Sleep, I've been told, is one of the best things an athlete can have, and I'm always up for taking full advantage of that bit of fitness trivia!

I was rather rudely awoken when we arrived in Cape Town by the sound of the Cape Town minstrels, a tap-dancing jazz band who'd been wheeled out especially for our pleasure. I tried to look delighted to see them before scooting straight off to the Holiday Inn at Newlands. Once I'd put my bags down, I picked up some of the local newspapers and found – a little to my surprise – that they were giving the Lions a hard time. One of the headlines ran along the lines of 'Soft Lions ready for the taking' and really had a go at our scrummaging capabilities. The headline didn't piss me off or make me want to batter whoever wrote the piece, but it did surprise me that a newspaper could be so upfront in slagging us off. That wouldn't happen in England, at least not to a rugby team, but it seems to be the South African way. They don't have much subtlety about them, either in conversation or in what they put in their newspapers. They're just a very blunt people, so I suppose I was subconsciously prepared to accept that in the papers too.

Whatever was being written about us, though, there was no doubt that being in Cape Town immediately gave us all a huge lift. You could see it in the players' faces. The next match was going to be a big game in a big stadium against a big team, and everyone was looking forward to the big-match atmosphere. We'd even been invited to the British Commissioner's house to celebrate the fact that we were in town, which wasn't such a bad way to spend a Thursday evening.

When we got back to the hotel, though, Fran had a word with me and warned me that it was possible that Paul Grayson, Tom Smith and Eric Miller might all have to go home. Tom had a bad neck strain and Eric had picked up a broken cheekbone during the Border game which looked as if it might be too serious an injury for him to continue on the tour. We were possibly going to be in the disastrous position of losing three players in one fell swoop. We immediately had to start thinking about potential replacements for the injured players, and after a wee bit of discussion we came up with Ben Clarke for Eric and Mike Catt for Grays as definites. We weren't really sure as to Tom's potential replacement but thought of a couple of options, including Nick Popplewell from Newcastle and Darren Garforth from my club Leicester. We weren't even sure if Nick Popplewell was still banned from international rugby after various misdemeanours, but we got someone straight on the case to check it out.

There was no doubt that the toughness of the opposition and the physical approach that the South African sides took to rugby wasn't helping our injury situation, but I didn't think we were losing players because we were playing particularly mean opposition. Some of the injuries just happened and the hard ground was also taking its toll on players' tired bodies. It wasn't as if we were getting mullered on the pitch. I was particularly concerned about Tom Smith, though. He'd come from nowhere to put himself right into contention for a Test spot, and to lose him would have been a big blow. There was another reason I didn't want Tom to go home. Apparently he was prone to sitting straight up in bed despite being fast asleep and staring at his room-mate with a mad, murderous look in his eye. Very disconcerting for whoever happened to be next to him at the time (rooming lists were different for each hotel we stayed in), but very funny for the rest of us. Of course, Tom was immediately nicknamed 'The Serial Killer'. We decided that we would hold off on making any firm decisions on whether he and the others would have to go home for a day or so, to see if any of them responded to treatment.

We trained down at a small rugby club called Villagers, almost in the shadow of Newlands, on the morning of Friday 30 May. The session went on a bit longer than we would have liked considering the fact that we had a big game the following day, but I felt that we had had a productive morning that had addressed some of the problems the Wednesday side had faced against Border. We actually popped in to have a quick look around Newlands on our way back to the hotel and, needless to say, everyone was impressed with the place. In actual fact, most of the rugby stadiums in South Africa are fantastic buildings, but Newlands is one of my favourites. The crowd feels very close to the pitch, which means that the atmosphere simply pours down on to the field from the terraces. When you go into the place you get a real feeling that this is the kind of setting where you want to produce your very best rugby. It was inspiring, even if the press conference that followed our tourists' visit wasn't.

I definitely got the feeling from this little meeting that the British press were very down on us after the performance against Border. I can't remember exactly what questions we were asked, but you could feel that the journalists were already losing confidence in us. I tried to be positive about the situation when I was asked for my opinion. I said that we knew there were certain elements of the game in midweek that hadn't been right, but that we'd still won the game and that it was onwards and upwards from there. I don't know how much the journalists believed what I had to say, though. In my experience people tend to be sheep and follow the commonly held viewpoint, even if they might have their doubts as to how valid that viewpoint is. There was a photo call and about five one-to-one interviews to be done, and I had to work very hard at keeping my patience while I was doing them. I could see that over the course of the next few weeks I might very well lose my rag with some of these folk and blurt something out that I might regret. For the time being, however, I was at least managing to play the part of the diplomatic Lions captain reasonably well. And besides, the bottom line was that I didn't really care what those guys felt about us. I knew that the problems we'd had could be worked on, improved and overcome. I had no doubt about that, and I have to say I consider myself a better judge of rugby than most of the people who earn their living writing about it.

I decided that the best thing to do to avoid any more frustration would be to get out of the hotel and away from all the hullabaloo, so I took one of the jeeps that had been provided for the players' use and went down to the Waterfront area with Simon Shaw and Richard Hill straight after lunch. We did a bit of shopping and got recognised a few times, but then again, that's not really too surprising. There were a few Lions fans starting to appear, with the first Test getting closer, so they were obviously going to spot us. And anyway, when three guys are walking around wearing the same tracksuits they're going to get some attention! We all had a bit of a laugh about it and carried on with our business. The extra attention wasn't anything we couldn't deal with, that was for sure.

It was an enjoyable little jaunt, but by the time the three of us had returned to the hotel it was time to focus my mind on the game. A team meeting had been called and we went over some of the basics for the following day's game: calls, tactics, set plays. I was feeling pretty fit and comfortable, which made me hopeful about the quality of performance I'd be able to put in against Western Province. I thought it was vital that we came out of the game with a victory, and if we could win with style then so much the better. A win would give us confidence and would also go some way towards shutting up the doubters. The mood in the camp seemed both relaxed and confident, which I was pleased to see. The win against Border, though not convincing, had been a win at least, and the lads all seemed to have taken heart from it.

I felt a little bit of personal pressure, though. The onus was on me to lead by example and turn in a good performance. If I didn't, then I felt that the South Africans would give us all a really hard time.

I sat down with Fran, Geech, Jim Telfer and Dr Robson to talk through the next day's game, as well as the injuries that various players were carrying. Tom Smith looked like he was going to be okay after the scare with his neck and Eric Miller was okay to continue despite breaking his left cheekbone in the previous game. He's a hard boy, that one.

The bad news was that it was decided that Paul Grayson and Nick Beal would be leaving the tour, although we opted not to make any announcement until the Sunday morning so as not to disrupt preparations for the Western Province game. To be honest, it was no great surprise to anyone that Grays would be going home; everyone knew he wasn't right. Nick Beal was more of a shock. I knew he was struggling with a few knocks, but at the end of a long, hard season like we'd all had, who wasn't, frankly?

That evening the decision was taken by Fran, Geech, Jim and myself on who should replace Paul Grayson, in what turned out to be one of the shortest debates on the tour. Losing Grays was certainly a blow, but hardly an unexpected one. When the squad was first announced back in England I thought to myself that we'd be very lucky to leave with all those players. Somebody was bound to get injured before we headed down south. As it turned out Peter Clohessey was the only one not to make the plane, a pretty low injury toll in my book. Looking back on it, Paul Grayson really wasn't fit to go in the first place, so I was mentally prepared to lose him. And, without any disrespect to Paul, there was another player we could bring in at fly-half who we knew wouldn't let us down. If you lose someone from a tour who's by far the best player in his position and there's no one who even comes close, then you really feel the loss. There was only one player in the party at this stage who I felt was in that position, and that was Rob Howley. He was the obvious candidate for the scrum-half slot going into the Test matches. With Paul Grayson, though, there was an obvious replacement in Mike Catt, who was touring Argentina with England. He could very easily have been in the original Lions party because there's very little to choose between the two of them. They're both good players and selection had simply boiled down to personal preferences. Probably about 50 per cent of rugby fans would have picked Catty ahead of Grays anyway. We all agreed that Catty was the man we wanted and we knew that we'd have to get in touch with England coach Jack Rowell down in Argentina. We decided to wait until after the Western Province match before making contact.

The sun was already starting to beat down quite severely as I sat down to breakfast on Saturday morning. I felt the heat would be draining during the game, especially as I expected the pace to be very fast, and having not played in either of the first two games I was a bit concerned about whether I'd be able to last. I knew that rest was the only cure for my injury problems, but there really isn't any substitute for match practice to get you feeling sharp again. Whatever, I'd find out soon enough what kind of shape I was in.

The boys seemed a bit tense over breakfast. This was a big game and I think everybody knew it. Newlands was only five minutes away and I could feel the atmosphere building up already. I personally couldn't wait to get out on the pitch and get down to business. It seemed like I'd been in South Africa for an eternity without getting to do the very thing that I was here for, and I was itching to get on and play some rugby.

Leading the Lions out for the first time was an experience that I'll never forget. The lads were all fired up for the game by the time we were sitting in the dressing-room, so there wasn't much need for me to go into a huge 'Fight them on the beaches' type speech. That's not my style anyway. But that doesn't mean I was any less honoured to run down the tunnel at Newlands and out into the blazing sunshine. I could have done without the bloody lion mascot, of course, but that was one chore I was just going to have to put up with. I knew that it was traditional that the captain of the Lions was supposed to carry the mascot, but I'd already arranged with Stan Bagshaw that I'd be throwing it to him the minute I ran on to the pitch, so I was only going to have to hold it for a couple of seconds at most.

The cuddly toy palaver was soon the furthest thing from my mind as the referee's whistle blew and we were under way. If I'd thought that the game was going to be tough, nothing could have prepared me for the reality of it. Within the first couple of minutes we knew we were in a game, and after 20 minutes it was getting *really* hard. I was absolutely knackered, worn out by the speed of a game that was being played at a hundred miles an hour and by the ferocity of the sun up above. Carrying my big frame up and down the pitch at top speed was no picnic, and if I'd been thinking that the initial onslaught from the South Africans would blow itself out, I quickly realised that wouldn't be the case. There was no doubt about it; we were shell-shocked by the power of Western Province's game. We needed to regroup and to pace ourselves.

Western Province played some good stuff in the first half. They dominated the scrum, wheeling us almost at will, which made things very hard for us, and they scored two tries relatively early in the game. I knew we had to rethink our game plan – and quickly. We had to dig deep and find a way to overcome the problems, show some character. Things were very physical out there too. John Bentley was having a running feud with the Springbok wing James Small, which a lot of people picked up on, although I didn't really notice it going on at the time. Apparently he gave as good as he got, which was vital in my book. The Lions had to show that they weren't going to be intimidated.

Early in the second half we fell behind by 21–18, but then showed we could do what a lot of people claimed we couldn't. Not only did we compete with Western Province physically, but we proved that we were dedicated to playing a fast-moving, ambitious handling game. Bentos ran in another good try to add to the one he'd scored in the first half and Tim Stimpson kicked superbly from both sides of the pitch. Rob Howley pulled something really special out of the bag to deliver a cracking pass out to Ieuan Evans, and in the end we ran out fairly comfortable 38–21 winners, something that really hadn't looked likely just after half-time when Western had their tails up and the crowd were really behind them. Their pack was supposed to be smaller than ours, but they'd bossed that part of the game, which worried me somewhat, but the fact that we'd managed to surmount the problems of heat, scrummaging and pace of the game to bounce back and win was very encouraging. It had been a really tough game, but one that I'd enjoyed very much. It had been hard, fast and competitive, with a higher standard of rugby than I was used to, even in the Five Nations, so the victory gave me a lot of satisfaction. Plus I'd come through unscathed as far as injury was concerned. All in all I thought that happy days were definitely here!

The press who attended the after-match conference, however, didn't seem to agree with me. They were still enjoying picking holes in the team's performance, which I thought was particularly negative considering the quality of the opposition we were playing. The Western Province captain, Dick Muir, had a different viewpoint, though, and was quick to praise us after the game, saying that they were both surprised and impressed by the speed of our game and the positive attitude we'd shown. Some of their players actually came into our dressing-room after the game to congratulate us and to tell us to ignore some of the harsher criticism we'd received in the press. They said if we played as well as that throughout the tour then we'd have nothing to fear in South Africa. I thought that was a nice gesture and a great compliment.

Where was the downside to the game? There wasn't one, apart from the fact that our shirts were falling apart. The numbers had started to come off some shirts during the Border game and some of the stitching had been tearing as soon as anybody put a hard tackle in, which had made us look a bit shabby in the two games. After some moaning Adidas did address the problem and had new shirts delivered very quickly.

The boys were naturally delighted with the win and everyone was up for a bit of a party in Cape Town. We decided to head for a place called Cantina Tequila to enjoy a few beers and had a rattling good night. We all felt we'd proved a point and had set ourselves up nicely for the forthcoming games. There were a few Lions supporters out and about as well. It seemed that the first set of fans had already arrived from Britain, had enjoyed the day's win as much as we had, and were all looking forward to a good tour. I hoped we'd be able to deliver the kind of results they wanted – the kind of results we all wanted.

CHAPTER EIGHT

Injury Worries

After our big night out in Cape Town, Sunday naturally began with a hangover, which is never particularly pleasant to deal with. I reasoned that I was allowed to feel rubbish, though, having come through my first game with a win that was achieved in some style. I decided that I'd best throw myself into a recovery session and shake my throbbing headache off with some vigorous exercise.

After every game the guys who've played the previous day always go into a recovery session, a two- or three-mile run with stretches or, like today, some running exercises in the pool and a bit of swimming. It helps to get rid of the lactic acid, the toxins that build up when you vigorously exercise your muscles. When I got back from the pool, I had something to eat, packed my bags, then lay down on the bed and closed my eyes, thinking I had time for a snooze because we weren't due to leave Cape Town for Pretoria until half-past two. I don't know where I got that idea from, though, because the bus was actually leaving for the airport at one o'clock! The next thing I knew was the phone ringing with a message that I'd missed the bus. The boys had waited for about ten minutes or a quarter of an hour, then shot off without me. This was hardly the kind of behaviour that was expected from the captain after his first game on tour!

Luckily the hotel manageress had a car and a kind soul and she drove me down to Cape Town International at a speed which the police might well have taken exception to if there had been any on the street that day! At the time, missing the team coach felt like my worst nightmare, but I actually managed to beat the bus to the airport and was waiting for the rest of the party when they arrived. I didn't think that being smug would have been particularly appropriate, though, so I simply tried to keep a low profile and mingle into the group as if I'd been there all along. Most of the lads didn't actually notice I'd been missing anyway and I could have got away with it, because I could easily have claimed to have been doing a press conference or some other official duty, but I decided to come clean and confess my sin. Tour finemaster Tim Stimpson immediately slapped a 100 rand fine on me, which I was quite happy with. It could have been a lot worse. I paid up within the week, which was probably a good thing seeing as Stimmo had his three henchmen on hand to sort out anyone who tried to duck their fine. The idea of Simon Shaw, Dai Young and Tom Smith coming after you with evil on their minds isn't a particularly pleasant proposition; it's much easier simply to pay up.

It was good to be on the plane at last, heading for Johannesburg and then on to our final destination, Pretoria. The place is quiet, about 45 minutes from Jo'burg, and it's got a small-town feel to it, not too big and bustling. There's plenty to do there, though, with cinemas and good bars and restaurants all close to our hotel, the Holiday Inn Crowne Plaza. This would be our base for the next 11 days and most of the party were happy to be there. Plenty of us knew the area a little bit having stayed there during the World Cup in '95, and you'd definitely choose to spend time there rather than in Johannesburg any day. To my mind, it's a lot more pleasant.

One of the first things that needed to be taken care of was getting Mike Catt over from Argentina as quickly as possible, so it was down to Fran to ring the England coach Jack Rowell at his hotel. I stayed in the room while he made the call, which turned out to be an awkward conversation as Jack was obviously not too pleased to lose his star man. Catty was playing particularly well and it seemed from what I could gather that Jack wanted to hang on to him for another week until after the second Test match against the Pumas.

The conversation was going around in circles and it seemed to me that Jack was really dragging out the discussion. We wanted Catty out with us as soon as possible to get him into the swing of things, and while Catty wouldn't have wanted to leave England in the lurch for the second Test, there was no way that he wouldn't want to come out and join us as quickly as possible. No international country should hold a player back from coming out and playing for the British Lions. I didn't really think there was much to discuss. The British Lions was the bigger tour and Catty should have been able to join up with us straightaway – and with the blessing of his team manager. I know in the professional era Mike would have signed a tour contract to play in Argentina, but even so, this kind of haggling was pointless. I understood that Jack didn't want to lose Mike, too, but if it ever came out in the press that Jack Rowell wasn't going to release a player for the British Lions, then he would have been crucified. And what would he have said to Mike? 'You can't go and play on the biggest tour of your life.' To me the whole thing was just silly and a waste of time. I haven't spoken to Jack about it and I probably never will, but in the end things did get sorted out and Mike was on the earliest possible plane to Johannesburg.

As if that wasn't enough grief for one night, Nick Beal's wife phoned from England saying she'd seen a story on Teletext indicating that he was coming home early. This whole situation was very awkward, because it turned out that there hadn't actually been a conversation with Nick about leaving the tour after I'd met with Fran, Geech and Dr Robson on Friday. I'd assumed that someone would have spoken to Nick, but at some point the management had obviously changed their mind about how fit he actually was. The doctor *had* discussed the extent of his injury with him, but no one had ever talked to him about having to fly home. Bealy had obviously then declared he was fit and the management had decided they needed him to play in the Wednesday match against Mpumalanga, so they'd taken a chance – which turned out to be the right decision in the end because he played through the rest of the tour without too much trouble.

This awkward situation with the Teletext announcement gave rise to two problems, though: one, it looked as if someone within the upper echelons of the party had leaked some information that they shouldn't have, and two, it looked as if a decision had been made about a player without consulting him properly about it. The whole thing was very embarrassing. I wondered straightaway whether Bealy would feel he'd been let down by the management, but when I spoke to him he was quite cool about it. To say he wasn't disturbed by it wouldn't be true, but he didn't need to go in for counselling or anything! He took the whole unfortunate episode in his stride and simply got on with it, which I thought was a very big-hearted and professional response.

Our first full day in Pretoria, 2 June, began with Jim Telfer calling a meeting of the forwards 15 minutes before the main squad meeting of the morning to tell us a few home truths. The harshness of his criticisms took us by surprise. Everyone was on a bit of a high after the Western Province match, where we'd scored some nice tries, but Jim wanted to keep everyone's feet on the ground by reminding the forwards that in some aspects of the play in Western Province, especially the scrummage, we'd been very much second best. Jim told us in no uncertain terms not to start thinking we were better than we were. 'You've got to face four teams on the trot now, teams that will probably be better than Western Province, and it's time to toughen up. Whatever adversity you come up against now, just get on with it. Don't whinge about the hotel, don't whinge about the food. Don't whinge about the training, the altitude or the refs.' It was a good speech, telling us to accept the country we were in and become a part of it, almost become South Africans, in a way, and play the game with their sort of ruggedness. He said, 'Some of you are like English tourists abroad. The first thing you do is look for a pint of Guinness, the next thing you do is look for an English fish and chip shop. The only thing you accept about a foreign country is the sun. That's no good. If you want to succeed you'll have to immerse yourselves in the culture of the place.' He was right about that and I was impressed by the sheer passion of his speech.

Jim's main strength is that he talks with utter conviction. Sometimes he gets so intense that he starts frothing – spittle actually comes out of the sides of his mouth! However he does it, though, when Jim speaks like that everyone responds to him. If a coach gets the tone wrong or says the wrong thing, then international rugby players will just ignore him, but Jim had a way about him that the players respected. He's got a massive enthusiasm for rugby, so much so that it wears off on the players. The only other coach I've known with the same talent was a guy called Phil Keith-Roach, who works on the England scrummaging. Phil's so enthusiastic about that aspect of the game that he took an England team that merely scrummaged to get by to a team that really wanted to scrummage and turn the scrum into a positive attack every time. He managed to get the England players to spend over an hour in a little room with a video machine going over scrummages from a single game without getting bored, which to my way of thinking was one hell of an achievement. Jim's very much like that: players don't turn off when he's getting into it, they turn on and improve. And, to be honest, we needed to. The scrummage wasn't going well on the tour and from this moment on we really went for it in the sessions. They became a lot more aggressive and very hard work.

The difficulty I was having was that despite coming through my first game okay, my shoulder was still giving me grief, which was seriously restricting my ability to train at 100 per cent intensity. The session that morning was brutal and everyone worked very, very hard, doing everything that was asked of them. I was only taking part 50 per cent because my shoulder was still sore, while the rest of the boys were working their knackers off. I felt a bit of a fake, just another supporter watching the Lions. I was sitting there watching the lads, with Jim shouting at them, and I could see their legs getting tired, see them going through the pain . . . and I was sitting there twiddling my thumbs. I hate being on the sidelines. Sometimes you know you've got to rest, and that was one of those days, but it was difficult at the time because I wanted to be out there doing it. Not just because I was the captain, but because *I* wanted to.

I was pleased to see that some of the players were taking it upon themselves to lead the others on the pitch. Keith Wood and John Bentley, in particular, were always keen to gee the lads up. John's not shy about voicing his opinions and some players don't like it; they think they're getting shouted *at* rather than encouraged, but that's just the way Bentos is. There is a fine line, though. If you're shouting encouragement, that's one thing, but if you're telling people what to do then that's another. I never heard Bentos say anything where I thought, 'Christ, can you just shut up now?' To me it was always good stuff, and if you didn't want to listen to it then you could just switch off. If it was aimed at you directly and you weren't happy with it, then you could just say, 'John, leave it out.' No problem.

I decided at the end of the training session that I'd have a jab in the shoulder that night in the hope that it would sort the problem out quickly. It was a bit of a performance, as I needed permission from SARFU, the South African Rugby Football Union, to have the two cortisone injections, so the tour doctor, James Robson, contacted them and told them what was happening.

Some people reading this might be aware of all the horror stories about sportsmen who've played through pain with the help of such jabs only to pay a terrible price later in life, what with crippled limbs and such like, but I was fully aware that the AC joint I was having trouble with is not a major joint that's in constant use and suffers major pressure. There were only five weeks left of the tour and this wasn't a serious injury. It just needed rest, but I didn't have time for that. The long-term consequences of my decision to take the jabs are probably of no real danger to me, and if I did have any trouble later in my career, there's a minor operation I could have to sort it out, so it's not a problem. It's not like having trouble with my knee or Achilles, although, to be honest, on a Lions tour I think I would have taken a jab anywhere to keep playing. That's why we have medical teams on a tour: to stop people like me making rash or stupid decisions. Having said that, as the game becomes more professional, who knows what kind of pressure will be brought to bear on those medical guys to put players out on the field when they shouldn't?

Still, now wasn't the time to be ruminating on such philosophical matters, because there was another evening function to attend, this time for Scottish Provident, about 30 minutes' coach ride from the hotel. It was a strange affair, too, held in a big private house with very few folk from Scot Prov in attendance anyway. Such are the occasional vagaries of putting on the blazer and representing the British Lions, I suppose. I know that I'd much rather be on the training field . . . or in bed. Which is exactly where I stayed the following day, Tuesday, our first day off since the tour started.

After a good, long sleep that made me feel refreshed again, I finally got myself up at midday – and felt a lot better for it. In general I wasn't sleeping particularly well, waking up in the night a lot, partly because of the shoulder pain which didn't seem to be clearing up very fast and partly because the hotel in Pretoria was on a noisy street. There were always people shouting and whistling outside very early in the morning trying to sell their fruit, which is pretty annoying. I decided to rest the shoulder completely, and spent the afternoon walking round the town with Richard Wegrzyk, our masseur, starting to turn my thoughts to the following day's game against Mpumalanga, who were formerly known as South East Transvaal.

Later on I had a chat with Tim Rodber, who was captaining the team. He seemed a little bit concerned that the midweek team had started to believe that there was now a split developing between themselves – the dirt-trackers, as those midweek players had been known on previous Lions tours – and the guys playing on Saturdays. Tim reckoned people had started believing that the side for the Test matches would definitely be chosen from the Saturday players and that the rest of the lads were already feeling a bit marginalised from the core of the tour. Obviously I was concerned that Tim should have a suspicion that people might be feeling that way. He's a very experienced player and a touring veteran, so his opinion was important to me. He was captain of Wednesday's team and had been training with them, so he could judge the mood better than I could, and he said that things had been very quiet. I wondered if that was because guys like Tom Smith and Paul Wallace were just quiet by nature, but then again they also had chaps like Doddie Weir and Jerry Davidson in the side who are a long way short of reticence, so I was happy to take his concerns seriously. I also wondered whether this downer wasn't fairly natural. We'd just left Cape Town after a big game against Western Province and now we were playing in a place called Witbank against a side called Mpumalanga, where everything was, to put it mildly, much more low-key. It would be almost unnatural if the guys hadn't had more difficulty raising themselves for that sort of game. I thought it simply made it all the more important for Geech to let everybody know that the Test side really was still undecided and that everybody really *did* have a chance of making it. Tim told Geech to do that in the team meeting that night.

A few of the lads decided to go to the INXS concert in Johannesburg that night, including Simon Shaw, who'd been drafted on to the bench for the next day's game at the last minute because Scott Quinnell had a foot infection. He asked if he was okay to go, and I thought: 'Christ, why not?' Some people could say that a member of the team was at a pop concert the night before a game and that it wasn't ideal preparation, but, personally, I thought it was better than being stuck in a hotel, thinking about the game too much and kicking your heels. Me? I stayed at the hotel. Possibly because I'm not particularly into INXS, but more likely because I was sulking with my bad shoulder.

CHAPTER NINE

Things Turn Nasty

I was very wary of Mpumalanga. They'd beaten Wales quite heavily in '95 and people had warned us that they were a good team that shouldn't be underestimated. They had a big set of forwards and it would be a tough, competitive game. At least we made one good decision, sending the team off to Witbank in a bus on their own, with non-players following on later in another bus. I thought it was a good idea all round. When you have all the squad on the same coach, the non-players are obviously much more relaxed than the players, and I know that if I've got a game I find their laughing and joking a bit of a distraction. It works both ways as well: if you're not playing, especially on tour, you don't want to be hanging around after a game. It can take hours for the players to get sorted after a game, while you just skulk around, and no one likes having to do that. With this system the non-players could leave directly after the game. It's not a particularly sociable way of doing things, but you're not really there to make friends, are you?

On the way from Pretoria up to the game, Fran pulled alongside our coach in a car. He'd just been to the airport to pick up Mike Catt, so he dropped him off and Catty hopped on with us. It was good to see him; he's a great player and a good bloke. I have to say, he must have wondered what kind of tour he'd just joined when the minute we got off the coach at Witbank our baggage master Stan Bagshaw came running out saying, 'Johnno, have you got your boots with you? Jerry Davidson's forgotten to pack a pair.' Fortunately I had a pair with me, because we were going straight back to training after the match, so I lent him mine, which were a size 13. They turned out to be a size too big – Jerry's a 12 – so he ended up playing in Graham Rowntree's size 11s. If we hadn't been kitted up to go training, then Jerry would have been struggling, so he was lucky. He didn't really get the grief he should have for this ludicrous behaviour, probably because he turned in a great performance. He had to so that he didn't get mercilessly ribbed.

The game itself was superb. If you ever needed an example of how to play a midweek game on tour against a dangerous opposition in a dodgy place, then that was it. We blew Mpumalanga away early in the game, racked up a 28–0 scoreline with Rob Wainwright scoring a hat-trick of tries and that was it, they were out of the game. Sitting in the stands you could feel the home supporters thinking, 'We're getting outclassed here.' It was really all over after the first 20 minutes. To be fair, we had a more talented team out on the pitch than they did and we should have expected to beat them. The only way you lose games like that on tour is if you let the crowd affect you. The home sides, especially the smaller teams, get very built up by the people who've come to watch and by the occasion, and sometimes that gets you into trouble if you let them have a sniff of victory early on. If you let them get a few points on the board, then you know you have to dig in and it's doubly hard to beat them. You need to kill teams like that off early. At the start of a game there's a lot of doubt in their minds as to whether they're really good enough, and what you have to do is to make that doubt bigger. On this occasion that's exactly what we did, which meant that I could actually sit there and *enjoy* the game, a fairly unusual experience for me. To be fair, I had enjoyed parts of the other games, but not that much, especially in the Border game where we got into a dogfight early on and looked like going down.

We were totally in control at the turnaround, but in the second half the game turned nasty, with a lot of totally unnecessary cheap shots being taken. It's okay being physical, putting big hits and tackles in, but Mpumalanga started going for a lot of off-the-ball stuff that was nasty and dangerous. When you've won the game in 20 minutes and that sort of thing starts going on you just think to yourself, 'Christ, let's get out of here now and go.' I saw some of what was going on, and I definitely noticed that our players were getting more and more pissed off with what was happening, stuff that went beyond the normal hard rugby contact. All I could think was that we didn't want to be losing players in this game, because there was no need. It's one thing getting injured in the heat of a Test match, but it's another getting injured in the 60th minute of a provincial game that's already well won. I do believe the referee should have read the situation better than he did. You had a touring team that was far superior to the opposition and some opposition players – not all – were just out there to cause some damage to people. If the guys who are dishing out the rough stuff persist, then you have to get them off the field, because it's a waste of time; they're not contributing to a good rugby game. What's the point in having three or four players trying to cripple some of the opposition? Totally, totally out of order. It was, sadly, no surprise when Doddie Weir was badly injured by a thuggish kick at his knee by Mpumalanga lock Marius Bosman. I remember thinking it looked bad at the time, but Doddie was running around for a while after it happened, so you never really know. After the game the doctor took a look at Doddie and knew immediately that it was serious and that his tour was over with immediate effect.

Doddie was obviously very disappointed, but over the years I've found that when you have a really bad injury you never really show your feelings that much. And Doddie's the sort of bloke who'd say, 'Ah, yeah, well I've got to get on with it anyway.' He wasn't in tears or pouring out his emotions about how unlucky he was, at least not to me anyway. I didn't know what was worse, that he was out of the Lions tour or that he'd picked up a knee injury that was possibly very serious. I think most rugby players are fairly philosophical about injury. You know it's going to happen, you've seen it happen to other people, it's one of those risks you take but don't talk about very much. What was so annoying about Doddie's situation was that it was so totally unnecessary. What that bloke did was just wicked, and it really, really pisses me off that there are people in the game who are prepared to indulge in that kind of thuggery. Doddie's my age, 26 or 27, he's got five years left to play rugby and enjoy the financial rewards that come with it, and it could all have gone down the toilet for no reason. The whole thing stank.

What was even more frustrating for the whole Lions party was that because the referee had actually seen the incident, Bosman couldn't be cited, so effectively he got off very lightly indeed, with a pretty insubstantial fine. Not even a ban.

For all Doddie's disappointment, though, I was delighted that Nigel

Redman got the call as his replacement. We actually decided on the night of the Mpumalanga game that Nigel was the man we wanted – and I wish I'd put 20 quid on him being a Lion back in March. I'd be a very rich man by now! The Bath lock has always been a willing worker and a man with a great attitude. Imagine how good he must have felt to be called up. Admittedly, Nigel probably wouldn't have been with us if Martin Bayfield hadn't already pulled out of the England tour through injury; he would have been the natural replacement for Doddie. There were other guys who would have been in the running too, but Paddy Johns had had an eye operation, Garath Archer was out too and Nigel – or 'Ollie', as everyone knows him – was one of the few second-row players who'd actually been playing in June. A lot of rugby players hadn't had a match in four or five weeks.

Whatever, we were happy to ask Ollie along. He's a solid player, we knew he'd fit in very well with the squad and he always rises to the big games. There was just the small matter of calling Jack Rowell in Argentina once again, this time to ask for Ollie to be released. It transpired that there wasn't a problem. There's a great story going round that after Ollie had received the news, he went up to Jack and said, 'Jack, I can't believe it. I've been picked for the British Lions.' Apparently Jack turned round, quick as a flash, and said, 'I know, Ollie. Neither can I!'

CHAPTER TEN

Losing

We put in another heavy training session the morning after the Mpumalanga game to follow the one I had put in directly after the game, and coming off the pitch I felt absolutely worn out. We'd been doing more heavy scrummaging work using a scrummaging machine, and I was having my doubts about whether we were using this thing to its best potential. It seemed to me that we were simply resisting all the pressure the machine was putting through us instead of actually attacking it and using the machine to simulate what happens in a game when you're going head to head with another pack. It seemed like this was nothing but a test of strength, and as a result it was putting too much stress on people's bodies. Before long everyone was complaining that they had bad backs and it took a while for us to figure out why.

All of this wasn't helping my shoulder any, nor my looks, for that matter. The scrummaging machine was rubbing all the skin off my face, which made me a very pretty sight, but the shoulder was what was really frustrating. I could play with it, but not train properly during the week. I saw an orthopaedic surgeon, who took a look at it and said it was what we'd thought, just a niggling thing that wouldn't cause any long-term problems. The earlier cortisone jabs hadn't been particularly effective, so I had another one in the hope that it would be more successful in settling the problem down. And to cap it all, I had a perforated eardrum after taking a knock in training. It wasn't causing me any pain, but all the time my hearing felt dull, like when you're coming down in a plane. With all my injury woes I really didn't feel up to going to Johannesburg for an official meet and greet with the British Commissioner, and luckily I was let off the formal duties along with about half of the squad. We just mooched about the hotel and had a look at a video of our Saturday opponents, Northern Transvaal.

I find videos pretty useful, especially if the sides you're watching aren't full of the internationals you tend to see on the circuit. Northern Transvaal looked quite good. They like to go fairly wide at the back, so we knew that was something we'd have to look out for. To be honest, I'd seen very little of the South African club sides because I don't watch Sky television, although we do watch a bit of Super 12 at Leicester when we have video sessions, to get some sort of idea of what the Southern Hemisphere sides are up to. I thought that, yet again, we'd have a tough game to deal with on Saturday.

By the evening I finally received word on the extent of Doddie's injuries. He'd been to hospital for a scan and the news seemed very grim indeed, certainly that he would be out of rugby for a very long time. Knee injuries are notoriously difficult to deal with, and the attack on his knee had been particularly hard. There were all kinds of ideas floating about regarding what the next course of action might be. Maybe Doddie's club Newcastle might want to take action against Bosman because he couldn't be cited by the Lions. Maybe Doddie could take a civil action and sue for loss of earnings. That didn't seem unfair to me. If your career is severely disrupted or even ended by someone who has deliberately hurt you, then you've got every right to pursue it. When I actually saw Doddie he was on crutches and it was difficult to know exactly what to say to him. I didn't know the extent of his injury so I couldn't say, 'Never mind, it'll be all right.' I just had a quiet chat with him. Doddie's a good bloke to have on tour and we'd miss him, no doubt about it.

We had a light-ish training session on Friday morning before the following day's game against Northern Transvaal, training on the pitch at the Loftus Versfeld Stadium where the game would take place. Yet again, it's a very impressive rugby stadium which inspired me to work hard. We did some line-out work, running through things on people's minds for the next day, getting a little confidence in each other before the game – nothing too heavy. Back at the hotel we were faced by the press for the traditional pre-game conference, where Doddie's injury was obviously the main topic of conversation; it was an incident that the press could pick up on and really go to town about. Overall they seemed quite positive about our chances for the next game. I think they were quite impressed with the way we'd dealt with Mpumalanga and were upbeat about the way things were going, which was probably the first time on tour they'd been that way. I felt that the South African press, in particular, had been very hard on us, making a meal of the weaker aspects of our game without being quick to acknowledge some of the good elements of our play.

Jerry Guscott and I were asked to do a TV interview straight after the press conference. Neither of us was too keen on the idea, especially when we were told that the film crew was running 20 minutes late. But when we heard that the interviewer was a former Miss South Africa who came second in a Miss World contest, well, who were we to refuse? As it happened she turned up an hour and a half late and she wasn't really worth waiting for, which serves us right, to be honest. She did, in fairness, ask a question that almost made the interminable wait worth while. She said to me, 'Does it help being a captain when you're also a player?' I thought I'd misheard her at first, because I couldn't believe she'd asked such a ridiculous question! I thought Jerry might have gone ballistic at her stupidity, but he was actually all right about the whole thing. He was talking TV talk. A bit of a TV man, is Jerry.

'Ollie' Redman arrived at the hotel in the early evening and it was good to see him. We both had a bit of a laugh about how unlikely it was to be meeting here in Pretoria. He said that it had only really hit him when he got on the plane from Argentina to South Africa, but I knew Ollie wouldn't be overawed by events. He's been around long enough to take anything in his stride.

I woke up on Saturday morning with my thoughts full of the forthcoming game against Northern Transvaal, knowing that this would be our most severe test yet. This was a top Super-12 side we were playing, and even if their five top players were absent, thanks to the Springboks' decision to withhold their Test-match players from the provincial matches, we had still set ourselves the task of playing three top sides in a week. The chances of beating all three of them were very slim, in my opinion. I knew that things were going to be very tough and I put our chances at 50-50, no more and no less. I'm a bit of a pessimistic bloke by nature, but I'd have to say that was a realistic assessment of the odds.

In addition, I hadn't felt that our training had gone as well as expected. It seemed we were lacking some of the sharpness from our game that I knew we needed and I couldn't quite put my finger on why that was. It might have been a case of everybody getting so up for the Western Province game and winning it, then doing the same again midweek, beating Mpumalanga well, that subconsciously we were thinking that these sides weren't as tough as we'd originally thought. Another game had come along and maybe we were now thinking, 'Well, we've just got to turn up and do what we do and we'll win.' What we should have been remembering was what we went through to get to the point where we could win the other two games. Whatever, you could feel something not quite right in the dressing-room before the game against Northern Transvaal. The anticipation wasn't there, that slight apprehension. You should always have that little bit of fear of going out to play, fear of what the opposition can do to you if you don't go out there and produce your best form and I felt that that healthy fear of failure wasn't there.

The minute the game began, things started going wrong. We stood off Northern Transvaal and let them get the upper hand. Everyone felt sluggish, especially the forwards. We didn't have anything in our legs and no one felt sharp early on. For the first 20 minutes I felt absolutely crap on the field, just struggling to get around the park. I don't know if it was because we had trained too hard in the week, if playing at altitude got to us, or even if it was a combination of both, but we watched Northerns play for the first 25 minutes, simply letting them do what they do; we didn't even get in and tackle. We tried to put the ball wide straightaway but it didn't open the game the way we wanted it to, not least because Northerns defended better than Western Province. We let them have the ball too easily and made all the mistakes we knew we shouldn't have done. Jerry scored a nice try but to be honest they were running the game and if we'd conceded more than the one try that we did in the first half we probably couldn't have complained. We knew we had to score first after half-time to be in with a chance, but we let them in for a very early score by Adriaan Richter. Of all the tries we had conceded on tour so far, that was the one which worried us the most, because it came from a scrummage where our back row was successfully kept away from the play, which gave our opponents the room to make the score. At that stage we were 25–7 down and looking like we were going to get a whacking, but we finally pulled ourselves together and came back to 25–20 with another try from Jerry and two penalties from Stimmo. We were back in the game and playing okay when van Schalkwyk intercepted a pass from Gregor Townsend and went through to score. I thought there and then that the game was beyond us and so it proved, even though Gregor almost made up for his error by running in a try at the death. It was too little too late, though, and, to be brutal, a 35–30 defeat was about the right scoreline.

I had mixed feelings about the defeat as I came off the field. If we'd been beaten by a side that had simply outclassed us, then I would have been worried for our prospects in the forthcoming Test matches, but that hadn't really been the pattern of the game. The boys were pissed off because they knew they hadn't played well, but we'd always been aware that we were playing good teams and if we didn't play well then of course we were going to get beaten. We'd made too many mistakes in the game; we hadn't been on the ball and we hadn't been sharp. I didn't think there was any point in getting too down about it; we just had to sort ourselves out for the next match. We'd been rightly beaten, but even then we could have actually won the game at the death when we had a counter-attack that looked like bringing a try, only for the ref to call a forward pass which looked like a very harsh decision.

In hindsight, a lot of the lads said that perhaps it was the best thing that we hadn't come away from the game with a victory. We were getting too carried away with our own success, thinking we were better than we probably were, and this defeat brought us back down to earth. Defeat was a bit of a downer, but I'd have been much more upset to have lost the Border game. The most important thing was that we knew what we had to do to put things right and we knew we could do it. And, more importantly, Fran and Geech knew it too.

What we couldn't put right was the fiasco which awaited us when the entire party went out to eat that night. There were 50 of us who'd left the hotel for what we hoped would be a relatively quiet get-together. Nobody particularly felt like partying after losing, so imagine how delighted I was to see one of those signs which read 'Come Down And Eat With The British Lions' or some such nonsense again. The restaurant was packed and we had to sit huddled round these little tables, right in the middle of what felt like a goldfish bowl. I don't like being the centre of attention at the best of times, and this felt like we had spotlights glaring in our eyes. We just wanted to get away as quickly as possible, but there were loads of fans who all wanted to talk to us. I always try to be polite to rugby fans because I appreciate their interest in the game, but I know I've sometimes got a pretty short temper when I'm feeling fed up, so it's hard not to be rude sometimes. I really make an effort not to lose it with anyone, at most pointing out to people that they're being rude if they're really getting in my face. But yes, there comes a time, maybe when I'm sitting down to eat after a game, when what I want to do is just eat and not be talking rugby if I don't want to and not be speaking to people if I don't want to. I know getting hassled is one of those things that you can't do anything about and you've just got to put up with it, but that night was the wrong night for anyone to be chatty with me. And, to make matters worse, I was especially grumpy because I'd got a whack on my dodgy shoulder in the last ten minutes of the game. To be honest, it was a pretty innocuous hit, but it caught me in just the wrong place so I knew I'd spend the next three or four days being sore again. I ate my dinner with a permanent scowl on my face and got myself off to bed as quickly as I could. Believe me, I was very glad to see the back of Saturday 7 June.

After a short period of rehab work in the pool the rest of Sunday was free, which meant that I managed to get away from the Holiday Inn with Rob Wainwright, Tim Rodber and Neil Back for a spot of falconry up in the Orange Free State. I think Rob had met someone during the World Cup who'd come to him and said, 'Do you want to do this and that, blah, blah, blah?', the usual on-tour banter. He met up with the guy again this time around and so we jumped into one of the Discoveries and off we went. To be honest, I wasn't particularly bothered about the birds, but it was a good chance to get out of the hotel, drive about a bit and get to see some of the countryside. When I got there, though, and the chaps started giving us this little display, I must admit that it was very good. I'd never seen birds like that at close quarters and this man had bred hundreds of the creatures. I quite fancied having a go myself, seeing if I could control one, but the birds are obviously trained by their masters and they respond to them alone, so that wasn't possible. One of the hawks took a duck as it was flying through the air; it sort of hit the poor creature and took it straight up. That was impressive. We must have seen every kind of bird: peregrines, hawks . . . there was even a black eagle perched in the back garden, bigger than a turkey. Not even the chap's dog would go near that beast.

The people up on this farm were really hospitable; they put on a very decent meal for us, so we sat down and tucked into some ribs and steaks. It was nice to be out and about, to relax, just wander around some paddocks on this bloke's farm. It was particularly nice to get away from the tour for a while. You have to keep some perspective on things and forgetting about matches, tactics and all the rest of it for a while is a healthy thing. Unfortunately, the rest and relaxtion was very short-lived, because as soon as we got back to the hotel we were greeted by two pieces of bad news. Scott Gibbs had been cited by the South Africans for punching Grant Esterhuizen in the Northerns game and would have to serve a one-match ban, making him unavailable for the Gauteng game. Despite feeling pretty peeved at the lack of immediate action against Marius Bosman for the Doddie Weir incident – a flagrant piece of foul play that anyone with eyes to see would agree was a far more serious incident – Fran acted the diplomat with reasonable aplomb, telling the press that we had a fair hearing and were happy with the outcome. This bad break wasn't so hard to deal with, but far more serious was the news that Scott Quinnell had an injury problem and would have to go home. This was a real shock to me, because I didn't have a clue that Scott was carrying any kind of injury.

I was told he had inflammation around the muscle that was attached to his groin and that he needed two months' rest. I don't know if it was just a wear-and-tear stress injury or if he got a knock on it, but it was a very sudden development, and out of the blue he was gone. Scott had been playing well and was a popular member of the team as well as a good lad. It was a shame when he had to go home without warning. Yet again one of our key players had gone and I wondered, not for the first time, how many more injuries we were going to have to deal with.

Well, we found out soon enough that we'd have to deal with at least one more. During the following morning's training session it was announced that Allan Bateman was also carrying an injury, which meant that Jerry Guscott might have to play again on Wednesday against Gauteng Lions (formerly known as Transvaal). It was a shame that Allan got injured when he did because, looking back, it didn't help him in his quest to win a Test place. But Jerry was probably even more pissed off than Allan. He obviously wanted a week off, which, after the amount of rugby he'd played, was fair enough. He was after a bit of relaxation, but we couldn't really play anyone but him in a key game like this one – although that didn't make him any more pleased. During training Jerry gave me a bit of grief, taking the piss, like he does, although he was quite funny with it. I didn't worry about it too much. We all know what Jerry can be like and we all knew he'd get over it.

The problem we had with Jerry was just one of a number that were posed on tour; selection was generally a difficult process. We played a game on a Saturday, then Jim, Fran, Geech and I would pick the team for the midweek game the day after, on the Sunday, then try to pick a team for the following Saturday's match on the Wednesday night. Obviously this left plenty of scope for people to get injured once they'd been picked, and drafting players in from Saturday's side to the Wednesday team would cause all kinds of organisational problems as far as set-piece work was concerned.

Such problems, however, were made to seem a lot less significant, because straight after lunch Wednesday's non-players, including myself, were bussed out to Soweto under police escort to take part in a rugby clinic for the kids in the township. What with kids and coaches and various other people knocking about, I reckon the numbers swelled to about 500, which is a huge number of people turning out just to see the Lions. There was massive interest in the day; I even ended up giving a radio interview on a mobile phone in the middle of teaching. Obviously now that the political situation in South Africa has changed so radically, it stands to reason that, whether in the short or the long term, the black population will begin to exert a much greater influence on South African rugby as more black kids take up a sport which for years they ignored, as much for political reasons as any other. The very fact that there's now a club in Soweto, the Orlando Rugby Club, is surely an indication of things to come. Imagine how good the Springboks could become with an entire population playing the game!

Soweto was weird. It's a big place and, obviously, there are some areas that look very dangerous, places you wouldn't want to get stranded in. It's not at all like the townships you see in, say, Cape Town. There you get mile after mile of tin shacks, but Soweto has roads and brick houses, even if it looks pretty chaotic in certain parts. And the most surprising thing? There are lots of fish and chip shops there too!

The rugby clinics themselves were enjoyable from the point of view of teaching the kids; again they had such great enthusiasm and a lot of natural talent. One of Fran's standard speeches was: 'It was tough back in 1974 when I toured with the Lions and South Africa was effectively only six million people – just the white population. Now they've got 45 million people to pick from they're going to be even tougher to beat' – and that's very true. I guess that how quickly the country can start bringing the black talent through depends on how seriously people take the development programmes. People aren't starting on an equal footing right now – some guy in Soweto is not going to have the same opportunities as some guy who's been to public school in Johannesburg – but there are some positive signs already. A few of the guys in the Western Province who are coming through seem promising. A lot of people are touting a black player called Jeffrey Stevens, who seems like a good player.

The coach journey back was especially long thanks to some nasty traffic jams, and by the time we reached the hotel I was hardly in the mood to meet with the management to discuss who should replace Scott Quinnell. Also present were Rob Wainwright, Ieuan Evans, Jason Leonard, Lawrence Dallaglio and Tim Rodber, who were invited along to add their input to the debate. The TV crew were allowed into the meeting, but that didn't stop everyone speaking freely about who they thought would add the most to the tour. It boiled down to a straight choice between the two Englishmen, Ben Clarke and Tony Diprose, and Tony got the nod. We felt that he'd been playing well for England in Argentina and had very good ball-handling skills.

England had finished their tour to Argentina the previous Saturday and Tony had already gone home, so we had to be really sure that we wanted him out with us before we called him up; it wouldn't have been fair otherwise. I had a chat with my Leicester mate Neil Back about Tony too. I was worried that although we all knew he was a good player, I still wasn't sure that he could handle the game at the very top level. I suppose it could have been argued that he only had to play the midweek games, but that wasn't the point. I needed to know that if it came to it and he was needed, Tony would be able to handle a Test match. With the injuries we'd been sustaining there was a very real chance he might have to. Backy's opinion is one I rate very, very highly, and he said, 'Well, I thought the same about him as you until I played with him, but now I'm not at all worried. He can handle it. No problem.' That's what really convinced me that Tony was the man for the job. We'd see him on Thursday in Durban.

Tuesday the tenth was officially a rest day so, unsurprisingly, I decided to sleep in. I'd agreed to be part of a Lions group including Jason Leonard, Mark Regan, Scott Gibbs, Gregor Townsend and Richard Hill which would go and sit in a shopping mall at lunchtime to sign autographs and earn a few quid for the players' pool. Everything which was earned through personal appearances went into the kitty, the players' pool, and was to be divided equally at the end of the tour, although in the end it was decided that rather than simply take cash we'd try and think of something more unique and personal to take away. Money would just go in with a pile of other monies, after all, and wouldn't really mean anything. In the end we all got a quarter krugerrand, which everyone seemed very happy with.

Mind you, we had to earn our money on this particular jaunt. The shopping mall was packed full of kids. When you're a British Lion in South Africa you get paid an awful lot more attention than you do at home. In many ways it's pretty flattering and it's definitely better than turning up for some personal appearance and finding there's absolutely no one there. That really is a nightmare. I remember that the England team had a book out called *Band of Brothers* at the end of the '96 season, and I was asked to turn up to do a signing in a Waterstones book store in Nottingham with Graham Rowntree. Now Nottingham is known as a very slow town as far as rugby's concerned, and all I could think was 'there's going to be no one here'. The book would probably make a nice Christmas buy for someone who was into rugby, but it was only October and I was just dreading sitting there in Waterstones with a huge pile of books and people walking past as if Graham and I didn't exist. Thankfully we had a little queue of about ten people, so we kept them there for hours. People were trying to leave, but we simply didn't let them. About another ten or 15 people came into the store during the hour and we signed a hell of a lot of other rugby books – or even non-rugby books – for them as well! It was madness, and after you've done one of those kinds of signings then you're just grateful for any kind of crowd.

Of course, any kind of public appearance can be fraught with danger, especially when someone's got a microphone in their hand. As soon as you see the dreaded mike you know that you're going to have to deal with a question-and-answer session, where any lunatic can ask you anything they like, usually something utterly insane. The kids who were in the mall just wanted our autographs, which was fine; it kept us busy. But, sure enough, someone soon opened up the floor for questions and the first one I was asked was: 'How do you think we can solve our law and order problem in South Africa?' What do you do? Try to go off on some half-baked theory about something which in truth, you don't know anywhere near enough about to give a reasoned answer? Or do you seem ignorant and just brush the question off with a flippant remark? In the end I just took my courage in one hand, the microphone in the other and replied, 'Well, that's not really a rugby question, but I think you should all sit down together, and together you can overcome your problems.' Oh dear. I knew this answer was making me look like a right prat, but under the circumstances there wasn't really anything else I could say. Needless to say the rest of the boys were full of sympathy for the difficult position I'd been put in – and had a good laugh at my expense.

But that wasn't the end of the little shopping mall of horrors. After we'd been signing for about 40 minutes we suddenly realised that the place was getting more and more packed. The more kids that came in, the further and further back we were getting pushed. Eventually we got pushed so far back that we had to duck into this little shop that sold suitcases, soft bags and so on. The lady who owned it was very kind, told us to sit down and said that she'd keep the kids out. We all plonked ourselves down very gingerly, so as not to ruin any of the displays of bags in this little shop. Well, everyone except for Ronnie Regan.

There was one particular display of soft bags that was about as big as a sofa, a real centrepiece, and Ron just came in and decided to launch himself onto them. Imagine one 15-stone hooker coming into contact with all these bags at high speed. Well, chaos ensued, the display collapsed and there was Ronnie lying amongst the debris going, 'Cor, I'm knackered.' The rest of us were suitably embarrassed and immediately said, 'Get off the bags, Ronnie.' So Ronnie gets up off the bags, sits on the corner of another display and knocks a whole pile of suitcases all over the floor. His antics were so ridiculous it was like a comedy sketch! Ronnie was lying there in the middle of the Samsonite bags going, 'Ooh, that's better', while I was saying, 'I can't believe you've done that, Ron. What are you doing?' But that's Ronnie for you. Disaster follows him wherever he goes.

After such excitement I needed something to calm me down, so I decided to go for a light workout in the gym with Jason Leonard. After getting lost we eventually found the place where I then discovered that my shoulder was yet again too sore to lift weights, which made me a very unhappy chappy. It was a good job that I wasn't playing the next day. I don't think I could have made it.

CHAPTER ELEVEN

Winning

The boys put the tour back on track with a thriller at Ellis Park in Johannesburg against Gauteng. The ground was a bit soft and damp – very British conditions, which made me think that the game could be won if we played to the best of our abilities. We also had to put the disappointment of the Northern Transvaal game behind us, get ourselves up for a match against what was sure to be a tough side and prove that we had character in the squad. Mike Catt was making his début, which was a big moment for him, and I was looking for a big performance from John Bentley, who'd had a poor game by his own high standards against Northerns and had been substituted.

It was no surprise when Gauteng started the game at an incredible pace. It seemed that this was the adopted strategy of all the South African sides, to come at us like madmen from the off and try to batter us into submission. They put us under a lot of pressure early on but, as it turned out, that first quarter of an hour proved to be the best rugby they played all game. Once we'd settled down it was a very tight match, very competitive, particularly around the line-outs but also right across the field. We probably had a little bit of luck keeping in touch with Gauteng. Catty missed a few penalties and we defended really well, but after an hour we were still trailing by 9–3. Watching this one from up in the stands was one of the most nerve-wracking 80 minutes of my life. I actually took my heartbeat during the game and it was over a hundred. I could really feel it pumping away. All the hard work we'd put into defending was made worth while by the penetrating attacks that put us back in the game, and while we made mistakes, we came through well. We knew we had to win and showed a lot of character to tough it out and get back in the match. When we finally managed to score a try it was a neat move between Will Greenwood and Austin Healey which let Aus score in the corner, a brilliant try.

Good as that try was, however, the moment of the match had to be the stunning individual try by John Bentley. It really was a special moment, watching him running from his own ten-metre line and avoiding what felt like a hundred challenges to go through and score under the posts. Not only was it a brilliant piece of individualism, but it came at a crucial moment, winning us a game by 20 points to 14 that we could very easily have lost. That one moment was crucial for the psychology of the touring party. It made us all believe that we really could take on the best and beat them by playing fast, flowing rugby. Bentos had obviously pushed himself right back into contention for a Test place, but he was just one of a number of players who were in the running. A lot of hard decisions would have to be made, especially in the front and back rows. Backy, Tim Rodber, Tom Smith and Paul Wallace had all played very well, Barry Williams was impressive and Catty did well in his first game; despite the penalty misses his general play was very good. Neil Jenkins came on and kicked well, which made for yet another selection headache. I thought the Gauteng victory was a defining moment, a real team effort and the first match where I really felt we'd got to grips with our scrummaging game. All the hard work we'd put in on the training ground had paid off and we fully deserved our victory. As soon as the final whistle went, the non-players got straight down to the dressing-room and we were all going ballistic. I'd like to see a tape of what the dressing-room was like after that game, although I did manage to take some photos which will be good souvenirs of a great day. The boys who had watched the win were just as jubilant as the ones who had played, which said a lot about the kind of spirit we'd developed on the tour.

Fran had said before the game: 'This is a key moment on the tour; we've got to win this match,' and I think he was absolutely right. If we'd lost to Gauteng straight after the Northern Transvaal game it would have been very tough to pick ourselves up for the rest of the tour. I think we would have started to doubt our own abilities, so to pull through and come away with a 20–14 win was a fantastic achievement by the boys who played. The game had been an evening kick-off, the first of the tour, so even though we got back to the hotel

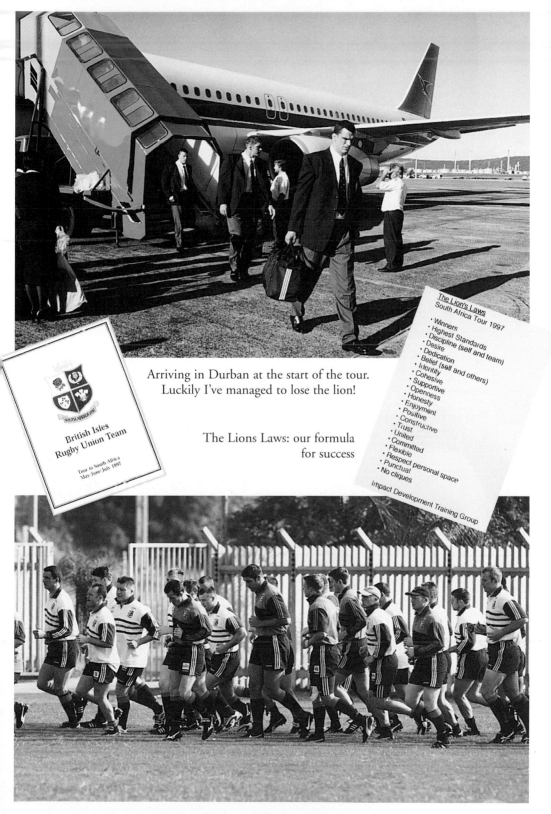

Arriving in Durban at the start of the tour.
Luckily I've managed to lose the lion!

British Isles Rugby Union Team

Tour to South Africa
May-June-July 1997

The Lions Laws: our formula
for success

The Lion's Laws
South Africa Tour 1997

· Winners
· Highest Standards
· Discipline (self and team)
· Desire
· Dedication
· Belief (self and others)
· Identity
· Cohesive
· Supportive
· Openness
· Honesty
· Enjoyment
· Positive
· Constructive
· Trust
· United
· Committed
· Flexible
· Respect personal space
· Punctual
· No cliques

Impact Development Training Group

Training in Durban: the first of many hard sessions

Jim Telfer and Geech: the masterminds behind the series win

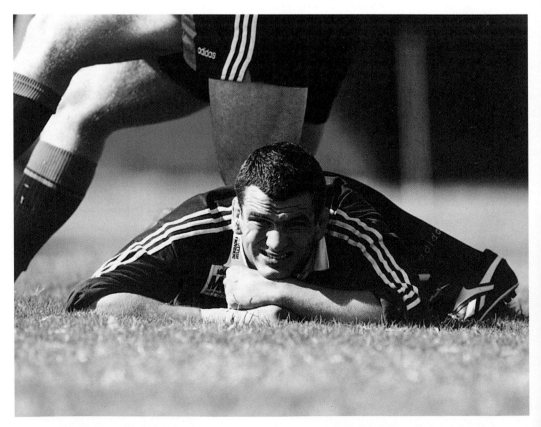

Feeling the pace during training. Was it my shoulder or my groin giving me grief? Probably both

The South African kids were delighted to see us at the Adidas rugby workshops

Not even go-karting could make me smile during our stay at Vanderbijlpark

We knew that winning line-out ball was crucial, which is why I look so serious here against Northern Transvaal

OPPOSITE:

(TOP LEFT) 'What? Me, ref?'

(TOP RIGHT) Leaving the field for a quick stitch-up during the Natal game in Durban

(BOTTOM) Looking a bit battered and bruised, but relaxed all the same, at the press conference to announce the team for the first Test in Cape Town

It looks like all that concentration paid off . . .

A proud moment for me. Leading the side out for the first Test, 21 June 1997

The brilliant Lions supporters always gave us a lift. This bloke looks well happy after our first Test win

The Big One. Spelling out exactly what we needed to do before the crucial second Test in Durban, 28 June 1997

Tom Smith, Lol Dallaglio and me giving the 'Boks some attitude before the second Test

Done it! Being presented with the trophy for winning the series at Ellis Park in Johannesburg, for many the home of South African rugby, made victory even more special

Fran Cotton and Geech both seem absolutely delighted. Me? A bit stunned, by the look of things . . .

pretty late, the boys were obviously in high spirits. Everyone was talking about taking on the Springboks. Everybody really, truly believed we could do it.

The following morning began a bit strangely, though, when I found out I'd missed the selection meeting for the next game against Natal. I'd gone to bed believing that the meeting would happen in the morning. I'd spoken to Geech earlier about the team and the plan all along had been to play what we thought would be as near the Test team as dammit in the Natal match, so I was a bit surprised that the meeting had gone ahead without me. I was told that people had tried to find me, but I'd only been in my room, which was a little perturbing.

As it turned out, Jim, Fran and Geech had their hands forced by circumstances and it wasn't possible to put out the 'Test' side they'd wanted to anyway. Allan Bateman had to play because Jerry Guscott had now played in two consecutive games. We would have played Jerry Davidson after a really good game against Gauteng, but he was injured. We could probably have played Tim Rodber at number eight, but he'd hurt his knee in the Gauteng game, so Eric Miller ended up playing at eight. Tom Smith was chosen instead of Graham Rowntree because of his strong performances. Rob Howley played at scrum-half alongside Gregor and they gave Jenks a go at full-back. I think after the way he had come on and played against Gauteng he had to be given a chance to play there. We had known all along that Jenks would kick his goals; he's so reliable in that area. The only question mark over him was whether he would be exposed playing at full-back when there were balls raining down on him from the sky. Even though I hadn't been in on the meeting, the team seemed fine to me. I didn't have a problem with the selection at all. I would probably have made exactly the same decisions, but I was still a bit pissed off with myself for not being there when the decisions had been made. I had a chat with Geech about it the following day, though, and felt better about the misunderstanding after we'd talked it through.

I don't know whether my state of mind affected that morning's training session, but I certainly didn't enjoy it that much and was happy to get out of Jo'burg in the middle of the afternoon and head for what turned out to be a surprisingly wet and windy Durban and our next base, the Beverley Hills Intercontinental at Umhlanga.

Preparing for the Natal game in Durban was hard yakka,

particularly the work we were doing on our line-out technique, because I was going to be playing with Tom Smith, Dai Young and Keith Wood for the first time on Saturday. Geech had given the backs the day off, which I thought was a good move, but I needed to get some practice in because in the two matches I'd played so far I'd been working with Graham Rowntree and Jason Leonard. I've played beside those guys for two years in the England set-up, so we've got our drills sorted out. Playing with Tom, Dai and Woody for the first time meant we had to spend about an hour and a half on the Friday morning just getting used to each other. Line-outs are really all about practice.

Again, I didn't think it was a great training session. It was a little bit long and it took some time to get into the rhythm. Simon Shaw came in because Jerry Davidson was injured and his ball wasn't working 100 per cent right. My ball wasn't working 100 per cent right either, even after we'd worked at it. It's difficult when you're training and things aren't quite going the way you want them to. Sometimes it's best just to leave it and come back to it another day. We were out there for a fair time and we still weren't really getting anywhere – which isn't that surprising considering it was the first time we'd worked together, I suppose.

The lack of cohesion made me a bit more nervous about the Natal game on Saturday. When you've got areas of the game which you know are solid then you've got built-in confidence, but when there are parts of the game you know full well are lacking then you're bound to be apprehensive. It's not that you don't trust the new guys you're playing with, but everyone has their own little ways of doing things. When you play with a guy for a long time you almost know what he's going to do even before he does it. If that telepathy's not there then that's when you get problems. It is only natural.

That's when you've got to be quite professional and say, 'Look, this guy plays differently. Just trust him, do your thing and don't worry about anything else.' Worrying's the worst thing to do, because when you start worrying about other people, that's when you start to make mistakes yourself. You've got to do what you do and let them do what they do, and if there's a mistake there, then look at it afterwards and try to wor'. out then what went wrong.

After training we went to King's Park to have a look around and soak up some of the atmosphere before the game. It's a very impressive stadium and has a good feel; it's a place that makes teams want to play great, entertaining rugby. I noticed that the pitch was soft and grassy, which I thought would suit us better than the hard pitches you often find over in South Africa. I knew that the next day's match would be an incredibly tough game, but I really felt I was ready for it. I even felt fit, too, which was a blessed relief after the problems I'd been having.

Trying to kill time and relax the afternoon before a game is often one of the hardest things to do on tour. Your thoughts are always on the game ahead and everything else seems like a bit of a distraction. A few of us took one of the combi vans to the shopping mall in the lovely suburb of La Lucia to stock up on toiletries – it's a glamorous life on tour – and ended up bumping into Springbok Ollie le Roux in a restaurant. He was a very big man who was, as the saying goes, eating all the pies. Jason Leonard knew him and he seemed like a nice enough bloke. We then headed down to the seafront to have a look at all the kids surfing and enjoying themselves. I think the people who live in Durban have a great lifestyle; it's probably my favourite place in South Africa. After all, there we were in the middle of their winter and the kids were finishing school and jumping in the ocean.

Strangely enough, we also met Paul Grayson's mum and dad down on the waterfront. They'd booked one of those rugby package tours and it was obviously a shame for them that their boy had already had to fly home. Not that they weren't going to enjoy themselves while they were over there. I know that if my dad had been on one of those tours and I'd had to go home injured then he'd still be down there having a good time.

We spoke to quite a few locals on the waterfront too, most of whom seemed very confident that Natal would have little trouble beating us. People in Durban always have a lot of confidence in their side's talent and they're very passionate in their support for the team.

The rest of the afternoon was spent back at the hotel going over some technical points for the game. Andy Keast used to coach Natal himself, so he obviously had quite a bit of inside knowledge on their players. There was nothing strikingly different about the way they played the game compared to how other South African teams did; they enjoyed playing off the back row a lot. We knew they were without Mark Andrews in the line-out because he was away with the Springboks, and they had a guy they'd brought in from Western Province called Wegner to take his place. Obviously we thought this could be a weak point in their game, since this would be his first game for them. I was always happy that we didn't have to face the Springbok players in the provincial games; there's no doubt that SARFU's decision to save them for the Tests made the games easier for us to play.

If I was in any way tense about the game, watching a documentary about Elton John that evening soon calmed my nerves. It was a very funny programme. What a prima donna that bloke is. There was one unbelievable bit where he was playing tennis on a court at some posh hotel, a fan waved at him and he immediately threw an almighty wobbler. He stormed off the court and was nearly in tears in the lift going up to his room with his tennis racquet. Once he got there he picked up the phone and screamed, 'I want a plane out of here now, into Farnborough, yeah, quick as you can. I'm moving my stuff out and I'm never coming back.' Weird bloke. I was watching it with Ieuan Evans and we were just going: 'Bloody unbelievable!' I suppose he's been a star for 20-odd years, so he doesn't know any different. He's just got too much money to spend. So thanks, Elton, for helping take my mind off the game. I chuckled myself to sleep.

Match day . . . and of course I slept late. I find sleeping the easiest thing in the world. Just put your head down and off you go. I know guys who can't sleep before games because of the nerves, but up to that point I think I'd only ever had one sleepless night in my life caused by worrying – and that wasn't about anything important either. Resting should be a big part of any athlete's life, that's what I always say. It's better than being out and about on your feet all the time.

The day was very warm and humid, so I made sure I drank plenty of fluids and stayed out of the sun so as not to lose any precious energy. The drive to the ground took longer than expected because of the sheer volume of traffic, which made me all the happier to finally take to the field. It really pisses me off waiting in the traffic before games; I get fractious. The weirdest thing was that we ran out to polite applause, which was quite unnerving, a bit like Wimbledon. I think that the people in Durban are a lot friendlier towards the British than folk from other South African cities.

The game started well for us and we even got hold of the ball for a sustained period early on, which hadn't happened up till now. Suddenly, though, all our plans went awry when Rob Howley went down in a ruck and came out holding his shoulder. Now Rob had emerged as one of the most influential players on the tour. His work around the scrum, his vision and passing ability, plus his great acceleration, added a lot to our game. When he went down I thought it looked quite serious, but I was desperately hoping that it wasn't that bad, almost convincing myself that he'd be okay. I walked over to check on him while the physio Mark Davies was treating him, and he was saying, 'It's just a knock, just a knock.' Rob was saying, 'I felt something pop out,' and I just thought, 'No, I didn't hear that.' I walked over and said to Mark, 'Look, if there's any doubt about this, just get him off' – and then walked off. I didn't want to hear any bad news. I should have noticed that Rob was in trouble because just after he'd come out of the ruck holding his shoulder I tapped a line-out down to him and he went to pass it off his left hand and couldn't, so quickly turned and passed it off the right. It had registered with me at the time that it was a bit odd, but I hadn't really thought about it properly. The injury was a real blow, but I think if we'd lost or played badly we would have taken the loss of Rob even harder.

Winning so convincingly – by 42–12 – obviously delighted us, though, and it deflected everyone's attention away from the problem. It turned out to be a strange game. Natal played well, but the match wasn't as tough as games we'd played previously, probably due to the absence of five or six of their key players who were tucked away with the Springboks somewhere. I did manage to get punched in the eye in the first half, though. At first I thought it was my nose, because blood came out when the fellow punched me – I'm still not really sure who it was who took a swing. It went 'splat', and I thought the nose was broken because I couldn't feel anything, so I went off and found that it was quite a deep cut by the eye and that I needed stitches. I had five put in, but the weird thing was that it was one of those punches that didn't actually hurt at all. It just caught me over the cheekbone and split it. I've been stitched after a game many times, but I've never gone off during a match before and it was a very strange experience. You run off the field and it's like a different world. You close the door of the medical room and there's a nurse and a doctor there chatting away, trying to make small talk with you and all you can think is, 'Fucking stitch me up and get me back on the field.' It felt like I was off for absolutely ages, whereas in reality it was probably only about eight or nine minutes. I got back on the field just in time to see Natal kick a penalty and for the ref to blow up for half-time, so it actually felt like I had two half-times in the game.

The boys felt very confident during the break that we could go on to win the game because of the quality of the defensive work we'd put in, and they were proved right. We started the second half very strongly, with Neil Jenkins kicking a number of penalties to put us clear, while Catty and Lol Dallaglio ran in a couple of tries towards the end to round off a convincing display. Gibbsy even managed to run over our old mate Ollie Le Roux – a bit of an achievement, that, and very good to see.

It had been a good game to play in and I think we all particularly enjoyed playing at King's Park. We were very much on top of Natal at the end of the game and I was particularly relieved that Matt Dawson had come on for Rob Howley and had acquitted himself very well. Natal didn't manage to score a try and we defended brilliantly. I thought that winning this game augured well for the second Test match that we were due to play at King's Park; we knew we'd come back to a changing-room where we'd already experienced an emphatic victory. Everybody was pretty high about the win but, obviously, still upset about Rob. I came off the pitch and immediately did a TV interview, feeling chirpy; I'd half-forgotten that Rob had gone off, to be honest. Then suddenly I remembered and asked how he was, to be told he was going home. It obviously took the edge off a fine Lions performance.

We all left the ground early to get back to the hotel, leaving the supporters to their barbecues. It's always quite a sight outside King's Park after a big game – a huge, sprawling mass of barbies and beer huts stretching out for what seems like miles across all the training pitches – and the good mood of the squad added to the general happiness.

Back at the hotel a court session was held, which I thought was particularly good timing. It was good to have all the squad members together to share in the victory, and I knew that everyone would be up for a laugh – and so it proved. Taking his role as the judge very seriously, Woody had gone out and bought false moustaches, tight T-shirts and leather-style biker caps for his henchmen. Tom Smith had a tight white vest on with a neckerchief and a moustache. Dai Young had on a tight black woman's top with see-through patterns, plus the cap and moustache ensemble, and Shawsy was looking very good, with his hair all greased back and wearing the moustache and a tight white sleeveless T-shirt. The three of them looked tremendously camp and they were christened Randy, Butch and Bruce, much to everyone's delight.

Woody stole the show for me, though. He was wearing a blond curly wig over his bald head, which was brilliant because it wasn't too ridiculous – a kind of '70s perm sort of thing. Sometimes on tour we've had a wobble wig, which people have to wear when they lose their cool and throw a wobbly. Once we had a pink one which was so obviously ludicrous that people didn't mind wearing it. It's when you wear a wig that could almost be serious and people take a second look at you that you really look an absolute jerk. Ronnie Regan was acting for the defence, and both defence and prosecution had hippy-style wigs on with false goatee beards. It was a cracking court session and pretty well everyone in the squad got had up for something. Except for me, strangely. I can't imagine it was because they were sucking up to the captain!

At the end of this very funny court session I still thought it was appropriate that I should give everyone a little warning about booze. Tim Rodber had had a word with me in the dressing-room straight after the match and had said, 'Good win, happy days, but we've got to make sure we keep things on the straight and narrow. There's a midweek game to think about now and the first Test next Saturday, which is absolutely vital. Let's make sure this win doesn't go to people's heads.' I thought that was very good advice and believed that I needed to say something to the lads in my position as captain, just to dampen people's high spirits a little. Tim has been around and he's seen a lot, and I think he was possibly worried about things that had happened when England had been in South Africa in the past. During the World Cup in '95, we went down to Sun City for a couple of days of rest and relaxation early in the week before we played New Zealand, and while at the time I didn't think it was that big a problem, looking back it was maybe a mistake. Certainly after the first Test we played against South Africa in 1994 there was a big celebration – much too big a celebration – and we never really recovered for the second Test.

How many of the reasons for that were physical and how many were mental I don't know, probably a bit of both. But Durban's a nice town, a party town, and it's a great place to be out and about. It's an easy place to get on the booze. After the court session everyone was on a high, so it was difficult, but I had to get up and say basically what everyone knew anyway. Yes, you can go out, no problem, but the doctor says four or five beers is the most you can have without it having an effect into the week. If I'd got up and made my little speech and someone like Jerry had got up and said 'Not bothered what you think, mate. I'll see you later', then that would have been bloody difficult. It would have been really tough to make the point. But everyone was cool. I'd talked to guys like Lol, Gibbsy, Gregor and Jase before I stood up, to see if they felt this was an appropriate thing to do, and they all backed me to the hilt. Guys like Jase like their beer, but everyone knew how serious this tour was and their receptive attitude to doing the right thing made my role as captain much easier for me to deal with.

With my words of warning hopefully in the back of their minds, the lads headed out to TJ's, which is a happening club right behind King's Park. I decided to go there for a couple, but when we arrived the bar was absolutely packed with Brits. It was a bit too full, really. Plus we knew there was a journalist from *Loaded* magazine there, so we had to be a little bit careful. You like reading the magazine, but it's a very laddish thing and they could easily turn something around and give people the wrong impression. Even a shot of a player having a quiet beer at the bar can be interpreted in the wrong way. Before you know it, it's not just 'The Lions have two or three quiet beers after the game' but 'Lions players on the piss'. If there's a big party scene with it all going mad in the background, or there's some pretty girl talking to one of the lads, then it can easily look bad, even if the situation is totally innocent. *Loaded*'s good, but it wasn't the kind of magazine we needed to be featured in at that time. As it turned out, though, I needn't have worried. It was the journalist rather than any of us who was thrown out for misbehaving, and when his article came out, it was actually the exact opposite of what we thought it would be. It just said that the Lions were all being really boring. That's not true either. We all had a great time, but we kept things to a reasonable level, or at least kept away from the press. I was simply pleased that no one ignored my request about taking things steadily and that a good night was had by all.

CHAPTER TWELVE

Back to Cape Town

Waking up on Sunday morning I was doubly glad that I'd only drunk the two beers the previous night. I decided to go for a two-and-a-half-mile run with Richard Wegrzyk around La Lucia, which was very enjoyable. I have good endurance so covering that kind of distance isn't a problem for me, just a pretty mellow way of easing myself into the day.

Before we left for Cape Town, though, there was a bit of a problem organising Rob Howley's flight back to the UK. He wanted to get home and have the necessary surgery to his shoulder done straightaway rather than hang around, so someone took care of things for him.

After saying goodbye to Rob, we took an early-afternoon flight out of Durban for Cape Town and found out that we were on the same flight as two Springboks, André Joubert and Adrian Garvey. Unsurprisingly I decided to sleep rather than indulge in conversation. I've got the art of kipping down to perfection – though not as well, I'll admit, as John Bentley has. He tucked up our media liaison man Bob Burrows beautifully on this particular flight. Bob was supposed to be sitting in business class while Bentos was stuck at the back of the plane, but in the departure lounge Bentos innocently asked Bob where his seat was. By the time everyone had boarded there was Bentos riding up front, fast asleep in Bob's seat. I must admit I thought it was really funny. What could Bob do? Make a fuss? Physically move Bentos? He just had to leave him there and sit at the back, which I thought was fair enough, really. If you can pull a good scam off then fair play to you.

By the time we landed at Cape Town again most of the boys were tired and irritable. The same jazz minstrels who'd seen us off two weeks earlier were waiting for us, but to be honest we just walked straight past them and got on the bus. I suppose we should have paid them more attention and they must have looked absolute prats performing for us when we weren't interested, but I was, I'm afraid to say, too grumpy to take any notice.

Back at the Holiday Inn at Newlands, in the shadow of Norwich Park, the first issue that the management needed to address was that of Rob Howley's replacement. There was a short debate about who should be the man and the names of Gary Armstrong from Newcastle and Andy Gomarsall from Wasps came up, but I think everyone knew that the Saracens scrum-half Kyran Bracken was the most logical and sensible choice. Geech told the press that Kyran had good hands and had been very close to making the original touring party anyway, which sounded about right. The bigger problem we had was actually locating Kyran. He was lying on a beach on holiday somewhere in Tobago and at first we couldn't get hold of him. I suppose it was tough on his girlfriend since he'd just been off in Argentina with England and she must have thought she'd get at least a couple of weeks with him, but what can you say? That's just hard luck and something you have to get used to when you go out with a rugby player. I think she actually stayed out in Tobago without him in the end, so I hope she had a good time all the same.

Sunday night's selection meeting for our next game, on Tuesday against the Emerging Springboks up at Wellington, about an hour's drive from Cape Town, proved a bit tricky again. We definitely had problems. There were a lot of players carrying injuries from Saturday so it was getting hard to get the right cover on the bench. Alan Tait was carrying an injury, but we thought he might have to play to help us out of a spot.

Whatever, we decided to forget about all the problems and go out for dinner at Blues in Camp's Bay, one of the nicest restaurants in Cape Town. Nothing ever runs smoothly, though, and the bus which was taking us all down there broke down on a very dodgy corner which meant that we ended up blocking off the whole area. The traffic was mounting up and there was even a fire engine trying to get past with its blue lights flashing and the sirens blaring. It was all a bit embarrassing really! Good job the food was good when we finally got there.

Our first day of training back in Cape Town on 16 June saw some pretty foul weather, which was particularly shocking after being in sunny Durban for a week. We were training up at the Villagers, a local rugby club right next to Newlands. The Tuesday team were working on a lot of kick-ups in the wind and were having a real nightmare in the blustery conditions, while the rest of us worked on tackling. It was a short session, but a fun one.

Robin Money, one of the top boys at Adidas, who'd manufactured the kit for the tour, had just flown in from London and I was particularly pleased to see him. Throughout the tour a lot of the gear that had been provided for us had been getting nicked in the laundry. I'm not surprised – it was good-quality stuff – but Robin was the man who could organise replacements. My agent Darren Grewcock also showed up and it was good to see him again and catch up on any gossip from back home. The interest in the tour seemed to be building day by day and I gave two interviews to British magazines, *GQ* and *Total Sport*, which both went well. Sometimes it's hard to fully understand the interest in what you're doing that exists back home when you're thousands of miles away, so it's always good to get a feeling for things from 'outsiders'.

More pressing than press, however, was the small matter of helping out Matt Dawson's girlfriend. She was due to arrive in Cape Town the next day, but due to a cock-up somewhere down the line still didn't have anywhere to stay. The last thing Matt needed was anything to distract him from the forthcoming Test match, so I had a word with our liaison man in Cape Town and asked him to take care of things for her. I'd been in this kind of situation before, where in the build-up to a Test match everything gets very fraught and it seems like there are a million things to do, so I made a big effort to get as much administrative stuff as possible out of the way early in the week. I was determined to sort out tickets for the game early so I wasn't running around doing it on Friday. There have been times in the past when I've been on the phone sorting tickets out the afternoon before a game and that's not what you should be doing when you're supposed to be concentrating on a big match. I certainly didn't want the rest of the lads doing it either. I needed players to be concentrating on playing.

My dad turned up at the hotel in the afternoon after travelling from England under his own steam. My parents are very cool and I don't mind having them around when I'm playing. I knew they weren't going to be hanging around the hotel getting in the way or expecting to see me and hang around with me all the time. They were just out there doing their own thing, which was great. Some journalist asked me if it's extra special when your dad's in the crowd but, to be perfectly honest, it isn't really. When you're out on the pitch you're simply focusing on what you have to do in the game and you don't change that approach just because your family's in the crowd.

After what felt like a particularly hectic day, I decided to go for a Chinese with my agent, Jerry's agent and the British magazine journalists. It was nice to get out with some people who weren't part of the touring party for a change. I didn't talk much, though. Too busy eating.

Unusually, the midweek game was taking place on a Tuesday rather than a Wednesday, so the next day's routine was a little different from normal. We weren't staying near to the ground either, so we all piled into the bus for the 50-minute drive up to Wellington – though not before I'd helped Matt Dawson's girlfriend Nathalie out of a spot. She'd turned up at the hotel but still hadn't got a room sorted, and Matt was already on his way up to Wellington. I had a single room so I just threw her my key and said, 'Make yourself at home. Order some room service.' I knew I could deal with her when I got back, and I couldn't just leave her hanging around the lobby not knowing what on earth to do.

The weather was wet and dark and the Boland Stadium felt like it was in the middle of nowhere. I imagined this must be how foreign sides feel most of the time when they come on tour to the UK, although I can't think of anywhere in the UK where the surrounding countryside is so spectacular. Enormous mountains roll off into the distance, seemingly carrying on forever. It's an impressive sight.

It was very noticeable at this game that the amount of British support had swelled considerably as the first Test approached; it almost seemed like a home game for us. It definitely felt like I was at home when I sat down to watch the match and suddenly realised that my old man was sitting directly behind us. I'm not, as I've already mentioned, the greatest spectator, and my dad was all bubbly, constantly chattering and saying things like, 'Do you want a sweet, Martin?' I was going, 'Keep quiet, dad. Can't you see I'm nervous?' To his credit, he calmed down a bit after that.

We started well and I remember Graham Rowntree going over for a try, which was both unusual and great, considering he actually ran it in from distance. Not a sight you see too often from a big prop like Graham. This turned out to be another of those games that could have proved difficult, but the boys gave a thoroughly professional performance. We let the Emerging 'Boks get back into the game a bit before half-time, but throughout the second half I thought we played particularly well and, importantly, defended better than we had done. To be fair to the South Africans, no player who had ever toured in a senior Springbok party was considered for this match, so this wasn't the strongest side they could have put out, but there were still some top-class players like Percy Montgomery competing out there and they were no pushover. Nick Beal ran in three tries, which was a really great effort from him, and Tim Stimpson kicked very well, but again it was the quality of our defensive work, particularly in the second half, that impressed me. The crowd, it must be said, were more interested in John Bentley, who had quite understandably become the supporters' favourite after that try at Gauteng. There were chants going up for Bentos all over the place and he was very funny after the game, milking the attention he was getting. There was no doubt that the fans wanted him in the starting line-up for Saturday's Test, so afterwards, even though he didn't run in a try, he said to Fran, 'You've got to pick me or 12,000 Lions supporters will revolt through Cape Town.' You have to hand it to him; it was a good line.

A 51–22 win and no injuries, then: a very good day's work in my book. We non-players all congratulated the lads off the pitch and then left quickly to get back to Cape Town and a training session under floodlights in the wet. More importantly, however, as soon as I'd finished training I went straight into a meeting with Fran, Geech and Jim to select the team for Saturday's Test match.

During the course of the next one and a half hours we slowly came to agreement about the side which would give us the best chance of a winning start in the three-match Test series. I felt that the best thing we had going for us was the fact that everyone in the squad was playing well. More often than not on tour you can immediately cross four or five guys who are not playing well off your list, but that wasn't possible in this meeting. Everyone genuinely had a chance of making the 21. The performances of players such as Rowntree, Regan, Leonard,

Stimpson and Back in that day's game meant that we had one hell of a job to decide on who would play in the big game at Newlands. There were some extremely tough decisions to make and we knew that a lot of the guys would be genuinely disappointed not to be in the 21. Making those decisions isn't easy, but I would never shy away from making them because it's a part of my responsibility as captain. It's part of the job. And I'd be doing no one any favours, least of all myself, by not making decisions and dithering about.

No doubt about it, I knew that leaving players like Graham Rowntree, Jason Leonard, Tim Rodber, Allan Bateman and John Bentley out of the starting line-up was tough. They're all great rugby players, but we had to pick the side with a view to who we thought would stand the best chance of winning the match on Saturday. We debated every issue when picking the side, but were especially keen to think about how the team as a whole would function. We needed to come up with a blend that would work, a team that would fit together perfectly, players who would perform to the highest of standards because the other guys around them would complement their own particular style of play. There wasn't anything that I totally disagreed with the other selectors about. Like I said, everyone was playing well, so you couldn't say any single choice was a bad decision.

Lawrence Dallaglio had been playing very well so we stuck him at six and then tried to get the right blend of players around him. We could have had Backy or Richard Hill at seven and Tim Rodber or Eric Miller at eight, so we had to consider what combinations to go with. We felt that if we went with Eric we couldn't go with Backy, and so on and so forth. Eventually we opted for Eric and Hilly in the back row, which was tough on Backy and Tim because they'd both played tremendously well. I debated whether Eric was the right decision. He plays with tremendous pace and skill, but for a Test match I wondered whether Tim's experience would help us more. Picking Eric was the more courageous decision but one which might well have backfired on us, but those were the kind of decisions that the four of us were there to make and we didn't back away from them. When we finally left the meeting we were all happy that we'd made the right selection. I was slightly concerned about leaving out John Bentley – his explosive style can always be a match-winner – but felt that he was still probably playing the game more in a rugby league style, which might not be suitable for this huge game. No doubt about it, though, it was hard to leave just about everyone out. Still, the decision had been made. The Test team would be as follows:

Jenkins, Evans, Gibbs, Guscott, Tait, Townsend, Dawson, Smith, Wood, Wallace, Johnson, Davidson, Dallaglio, Miller, Hill.

We'd decided even before we'd left England that players would be told whether they'd been selected or not by getting a note slipped under their doors the morning after selection, so giving everybody a chance to collect their thoughts before the official announcement was made. Fran and Geech insisted it was vital that nobody felt that this was the end of their Test chances and that team spirit was kept intact. We felt the privacy of the note and the time each player would have to take the information in would help towards that end. With five games left, two midweeks and three Tests, we wanted everyone to stay focused on the task at hand. To give full credit to Fran, he was very good at understanding the sensitivities of the players. Often you didn't even really notice Fran lurking in the background, but he was very sharp at picking up on the little things that matter. He was in a good position as well. As a former player himself, no current player could turn round and say, 'What do you know? You haven't been through this. You don't know what it's like.' Fran had done all this and more.

By the time I'd woken on Wednesday morning from a fitful night's sleep, the squad had been informed of the line-up for the Test match. The idea was that we'd split up into groups and talk through our feelings about what had been decided. There were two or three guys who'd made the side and two or three who hadn't in my group, which could have made things a bit awkward. As it turned out, everyone had already come to terms with the decisions that had been made and there were no signs of tension at all. There wasn't really a need to worry about anyone, so we just went off and had a cup of tea together.

CHAPTER THIRTEEN

Preparing for the Big One

Once everyone had dealt with their news about the Test side in whatever way they saw fit, the entire squad left Cape Town for a day's training up in Stellenbosch, which I think was specifically designed to take everyone's mind off selection. I slept all the way there – which was probably just as well for everyone else, as I was tired and grouchy and feeling a bit poorly for some reason.

We started the first session with Geech wanting to do some short line-outs and some contact defence. It was quite a brutal session really; everyone was going for it. Then Jim took the forwards for another session which was also very physical. Someone stood on Paul Wallace's knee; I think it was Jerry Davidson, who actually makes a habit of injuring his team-mates. He injured Gregor in one game, when Gregor was on the floor and Jerry came in and caught him with his boot. I think he might have stood on someone's head too, possibly Rob Wainwright's. He's a full-on, 100 per cent player who gives everything he's got at all times, even playing when he's injured. Sometimes you have to literally drag Jerry off the pitch.

As a result of his 'enthusiasm', though, Wally was out of the session and so Jason Leonard had to fill in, even though he'd played in Wellington the previous day. It wasn't very good. I don't think it was a particularly great scrummaging session, especially not before a Test match. We had lunch at 1 p.m. and obviously couldn't have any wine because it was the Wednesday before a big game and, anyway, we had to train again in the afternoon. We were sitting around feeling all mucky and dirty, we couldn't have a shower and we were just waiting to go out training again. We managed to get through the afternoon session and a full day's training before the first Test was reached. It was a shame that the day wasn't particularly enjoyable. Stellenbosch is a lovely little spot, but we didn't really get the most out of it and most of us were glad to leave.

On our return to the hotel in Cape Town I had a very awkward conversation with Mark Regan, who was very upset not to have even made the bench for Saturday's game. He'd gone out on tour competing with Keith Wood for a Test spot and now wasn't even in the 21 for the match. I understood his disappointment and I think what made things worse for Ronnie were the expectations of everyone back home, who fully anticipated him being in the starting line-up. He wanted to speak to the management about why he'd been left out, but I think he felt a bit awkward about how to approach Fran or Geech, so he came to me. He asked me to have a word on his behalf, but I wasn't going to lie and say I'd see what I could do. To be honest, I couldn't give him much joy. I explained that Keith Wood had been chosen and Barry Williams was on the bench because we thought those two players gave the team an extra dimension about the park. Woody had been more of an impact player than Mark on the tour so far and there was no way I could make that information sound any more palatable to him.

I think Ronnie could have lived with being on the bench, but he didn't like not even getting that far; he felt embarrassed about being third choice and losing face. As I said to him, 'We've got three guys in one position. If one is playing the Saturday games, then someone isn't going to play for a fortnight and, basically, he's lost his position.' Ronnie felt he'd lost out and that he wouldn't get a chance to play until probably the penultimate game of the tour which, as it turned out, was quite right. He was very disappointed but, to give him his due, his attitude on the training field was never less than first class. That was one of the most difficult conversations I've ever had on a tour. If someone comes to you with a problem, it's nice to say, 'I'll sort that out for you, no problem,' but there was no good news for Ronnie. It was tough on him, because I couldn't give him anything to cheer him up.

To add to my woes, shortly after my conversation with Ronnie I found out that Eric Miller had come down with flu, which would mean we'd have to rethink our Test plans if it got worse. I spoke to him about it and he said he had good periods when he felt okay, but then sometimes he simply had no energy at all. He knew that it wouldn't be right to take the Test place knowing that he might very well only be able to give half his best. Eric was obviously upset and disappointed at missing his big chance, but he also realised that he simply wasn't right. I was upset for him too, because he'd made a big impression on me since he arrived at Leicester – and not just on the rugby field. Eric can be a real lovable eccentric (this is a man who freezes his potatoes!), but even he wasn't mad enough to pretend that he could go out there and play when he was feeling crap; he knew he'd end up letting everyone down. So Tim Rodber came in, stronger in some areas of his game but without Eric's pace. It had been touch and go with me as to who should have had that slot anyway, so I wasn't unduly concerned and slept soundly. Of course.

Geech allowed us to start Thursday's light morning training session a little bit later after the exertions of the previous day up in Stellenbosch, but the lads were obviously still tired and the session was laboured, with plenty of mistakes. I wasn't too concerned and returned to the hotel to be greeted by the media swarming all over the place ready for the press conference, which I had to go into immediately. The place was buzzing with excitement and it seemed like the entire world had suddenly arrived in Cape Town ready for the big game. Even Emlyn Hughes was milling about the place. I couldn't help but wonder what the hell he was doing there, but sitting in the press conference soon took my mind off such trivia! The questions were obviously about the side that had been chosen, but there wasn't really much to say. We'd picked what we thought was the best team available and we all believed it was the side which gave us the best chance of victory. People talked about the South African team, but the Springboks had been very upfront about selection by announcing their side early in the week. There weren't any surprises there. All the big names were in the team: Joubert, Small, Honiball, du Randt, Drotske, van der Westhuizen and so on and so forth. It looked like a strong side, but I hadn't exactly been expecting them to pick a weak one! I said that the game would be our biggest test of the tour, but that our preparation had been good and that we were ready to accept the challenge.

After the conference I managed to get out of the hotel and went to a beach with a great view of Cape Town and Table Mountain to do a photo shoot. To be honest, anything was preferable to hanging around with the media everywhere, and I began dreaming about how nice it would be to come back here on Sunday and spend the day lazing about.

I managed to avoid the press when I got back to the hotel, in time for a video meeting at 7 p.m. We had a look at some footage of the Springboks against Tonga and paid particular attention to some of their key players: van der Westhuizen, du Randt, Kruger, Joubert. I didn't see anything in the pieces of video action that made me think, 'Christ, they play differently from any other rugby side I've come up against.' I saw some good stuff, of course, but if you *let* the South Africans play, then they *are* going to look brilliant. I still felt confident. We were playing some good rugby, rugby that was a little bit special and of a higher quality than some people thought we could produce. Maybe even of a better quality than we ourselves thought we were capable of. We couldn't really have asked for a better build-up. The only problems we'd had were with injuries, which were obviously out of our control. Why was there any reason to be worried about our chances? I finally hit the hay on Thursday night believing that we had as good a chance as we ever would have of coming away with a win on Saturday.

After sleeping in I decided to spend the first part of the rest day getting my hair cut. I hate it when it starts to get even slightly long. When you're on tour, you're getting wet through training and washing your hair all the time and you really don't need long hair. I just nipped down the road from the hotel to a hairdresser's that's virtually opposite the ground, one that I'd spotted on the way back from somewhere or other one day. People spotted me from their cars and were honking their horns and waving, or winding their windows down and shouting for the 'Boks. It suddenly really, really dawned on me just what a huge game this was going to be. I needed something to take my mind off it, so the crazy woman in the hairdresser's was just what I needed! This lady was as mad as a goose and was telling me that she wanted to shave my head for the big day. Now I know I said I didn't like my hair getting long, but this was going too far. I couldn't go for that; I'd have looked an absolute prat. I told her that I wasn't into getting my head scalped before a game, it was as simple as that. I knew that there had been a craze amongst the lads for getting their heads shaved recently. Matt Dawson had done it when it was announced he'd made the Test side. Austin Healey and Will Greenwood did theirs too, I think. Woody's bald as a coot anyway and Ollie Redman's had nothing on top for years, but it doesn't suit me, especially not before a big game. Besides, there was a fellow in the next chair who had an absolute disaster going on on top of his head, which provided me with more than enough comedy for one morning. I didn't need to contribute a ludicrous haircut of my own.

In the afternoon Geech unveiled his own, idiosyncratic way of preparing us for the game – he took the 21 who'd been chosen to the nearby Botanical Gardens for a cup of tea. Tea and scones, in fact. Geech wanted everyone to get together at some stage during the day because he believes that when you're together it focuses your minds. Of course, the boys started to take the piss out of the idea, but it was all right, to be fair. It was nice to get together – and keep out of the way of the media, of course.

After yet more sleep we gathered for a team meeting at 6.30 p.m. Geech had got somebody to put a compilation tape together of some of our best tries, hits and attacks of the tour. It was good to see all the highlights again – set to music actually – and it gave the boys a definite lift. The night before a big match the team meeting can be quite a tense affair, but Geech just brought the tape out, saying he'd asked someone back home to sum up what the British Lions had meant to people back in Britain so far and they'd put this video together for us. It was a good moment. I think that one of the pieces of music used was 'Wonderwall' by Oasis, which had almost been turned into the tour anthem. We sang along to it on the bus when it came on the radio, and whenever we went out to warm up for a game, we'd get them to play 'Wonderwall' over the Tannoy at some point. It's not a particular favourite of mine, but it's one of those rock songs that goes well with rugby play.

At the meeting Geech also stressed everything we'd gone through during the tour so far, the whole ethos of how we were playing the game and what we wanted to do. Holding on to the ball was a big issue. As he said, we might go through three or four phases of play, maybe even go backwards on two or three of them, but as long as we had the ball then eventually we were going to get at the opposition when their defence wasn't organised. Then we could get behind them, hit top pace and go for a score. Defensively, he urged us to keep a shape and a pattern, to cover the blind sides, keep an eye on them and not let their back-row guys run at us off their backs. We shouldn't allow their scrum to get a tighter wheel so they could take off the back row. Geech then asked a player from each section of the team to go through the key things that we needed to do. I spoke for the front five and stressed the importance of the scrummage and our competitiveness and will to win. I felt good about what was happening at this point because I sensed that there was a tremendous feeling and attitude in the whole squad. I didn't feel that the Test 21 was removed from the rest of the lads and I thought that when we took to the field at Newlands we'd feel like we were playing for everyone. One of Geech's little sayings that he came out with at the very start of the tour was: 'The only guys who are ever going to believe in us truly, 100 per cent, are yourselves and your immediate families. They are the only people who are ever going to really believe in you. That's it. When you go out there, think that you're playing just for those people.' I thought Geech's speech really hit just the right tone. He didn't get the players overpsyched or overemotional. He just made us believe that we could do the job.

After the meeting broke up I went to the cinema to see *The Fifth Element*, starring Bruce Willis, which I thought was a bit poncey, to be honest, and then I went to bed. I didn't sleep well because the wind was making a lot of noise, so I had a chance to think about the match in the dark, in private. I was probably awake until half-past two and I couldn't help but feel tense, which wasn't a particularly pleasant feeling. It was right and proper to feel that way, all the same. You think about any big match that's coming up and you should feel nervous. And if you don't feel nervous before a game then I believe there's something wrong. It's the first time I've ever actually lost sleep, though!

CHAPTER FOURTEEN

A Famous Victory

Running on to the pitch at Newlands as captain for this, the first Test, was a very big moment for me. There was a huge crowd in the stadium, with plenty of support for the Lions, but, to be honest, I didn't really notice any of that too much. I think there's so much pressure building up by the time that you're changed and finally out on the pitch that all you want to do is get on with the game, not soak up the atmosphere. It's a tense moment, the big face-off. You run out and they run out, they look at you and you look at them, they look at you in the line-up, they sing their anthem, and all that time the pressure's building to an intensity that's almost white hot. Of course, being the Lions we didn't have a national anthem, although I suggested they should play 'Champagne Supernova' by Oasis, just because I really like it. In the end we simply decided not to bother and stood listening to the opposition's song. The new South African anthem seemed a bit odd, a mixture of the old marching sound and a new piece of traditional African music. None of their players seemed to know the words, which was great from our point of view. We just started winding each other up, saying, 'They don't know the words, they don't even know the words. They're jokers, this lot!' Tim Rodber was getting himself psyched up by standing there screaming at them which I loved – and then we were ready to kick off.

We kicked the ball straight into touch, which wasn't the best thing we could have done. Then immediately afterwards we got a first scrummage at halfway and they absolutely blitzed us, driving hard and rolling us backwards. We were rocked back on our heels right from the off and within two or three minutes of that first scrum the Springboks put a good kick into the corner. Then we lost the line-out on our throw-in, which did absolutely nothing for our morale. It was just about the worst start we could have had. After the match I blamed Woody for throwing badly at the line-out and Woody blamed me for the problems we'd had. He said afterwards that he couldn't blame himself because if he'd done that then he would have been thinking about it for the rest of the game and that would ruin his performance, so he had to blame me and I had to take the rap. Paul Wallace then got penalised for collapsing a scrum, Edrich Lubbe planted the ball firmly between the posts and we were 3–0 down before we'd even handled the ball properly.

Things seemed to be going from bad to worse for us and all I wanted us to do was to get hold of the ball for a second and make them start tackling us. I was screaming at the top of my voice, trying to get the boys to believe in themselves and get back into the match. At that point we really needed something to break for us, because the 'Boks were absolutely dominating us in all areas of the game. There was a tremendous atmosphere at this stage because the home supporters knew their side had made a blistering start and the noise was absolutely deafening. It was very difficult to communicate with someone on the pitch who was anything more than a few yards away from you, but we knew we simply had to get back in the game after a crap start. We'd allowed them to do just what they wanted to do to us, and we hadn't done anything like what we wanted to do to them.

We kept telling each other that the Springboks' ferocious start was like a flash thunderstorm, that it would blow itself out quickly, but while that's what I was telling the other lads, the truth was that I wasn't convinced. During most of the games on this tour so far we'd seen that teams were forced to step off the gas after about 20 minutes, that it was impossible to keep up such a furious pace for a prolonged period, but this was a Test match. Maybe the adrenaline would carry them through that 20-minute barrier. Maybe it would keep them going for the whole match and we'd never get the chance to fight our way back into it. It crossed my mind that maybe today wouldn't be our day; we'd been so thoroughly outplayed in the opening period. If we'd let them continue to dominate us for the first half-hour, the Springboks would have had so many points on the board that we would have been out of the game completely, but our defence showed tremendous determination, pulled together and then helped the rest of the side to start getting some play going. We started to get some good scrummages in and suddenly, from having been completely overrun, we were right back in the game.

Our confidence returned pretty quickly. I think that the key was that we never let them get out of reach early. Jenks kicked us level when Strydom came in on the wrong side of the ruck, then he kicked us back to within a couple of points after Os du Randt had driven over from about five metres for a South African try. Jenks was so solid with his kicking that it was fantastic, and he actually sent us in a point ahead at half-time, 9–8, with three brilliantly executed penalties. The Springboks were ruining a lot of their good forward play with indiscipline, giving penalties away which we just said 'Thank you very much' for and slotted over. We didn't give penalties away as a tactic. When they had the ball and were attacking, they'd win three or four phases well, but we just hung in there, working hard to defend. When we had the ball and were moving forward they'd give a penalty away very quickly. It looked like they had a lot of pressure on us, but we were scoring a lot more freely. You can't defend a guy kicking a ball over the posts and after that initial period we were confident in our own defensive work. If we were ever in doubt about getting penalised, we simply let them have the ball, made sure we didn't give a penalty away and kept tackling. The 'Boks seemed happy to put pressure on in the ruck and maul and played a borderline game where they could give penalties away or turn the ball over. We adopted a different approach. I wouldn't say the way they were playing was particularly more adventurous, it was just a different way of doing things. Some of the penalties they gave away were silly and needless. They put too much pressure on the ball and I could see that as the game wore on we got much, much stronger.

We had a rotten start to the second half in the same way we had in the first. The Springbok substitute Russell Bennett, who had come on to replace Lubbe, broke through after a very good run from their captain Gary Teichmann, and again they could have won the game if we'd let them take it away from us at that point. We were making too many mistakes while trying to hold on to the ball now, but again we toughed it out. Jenks slotted another penalty about halfway through the second half to keep us in touch at 16–15 and then, in one glorious moment, Matt Dawson managed to break through, shoot down the right-hand side and score. It was an amazing try and an amazing moment for Daws; it was obviously just meant to be his night. Considering that he wouldn't have been in the starting line-up if Rob Howley had been fit, it was an incredible score for him. He faked an overhead pass and two or three Springboks put their hands up and seemed almost to stop, so he just kept on going and ran it in. It was weird. The whole thing almost looked too telegraphed for anyone to have fallen for it, but if someone puts their hands up to pass the ball, your immediate reaction is to put your hands up to stop them doing it. It was a brilliant moment and the try came at a great time psychologically, with only eight minutes to go.

The try really rocked South Africa back on their heels and made them throw caution to the wind and take the game to us, which meant that their defence wasn't going to be as solid. It just gave us a bit more room to move going forward and, sure enough, things opened up for us again right at the death; Jenks gave a neat pass to Alan Tait and he went through to score in the opposite corner to Daws and clinch the game 25–16. Taits gave a double pistol salute to the South African fans behind the goal, who were already leaving in droves. It was a great moment and within seconds the referee had blown up for full-time. I greeted the end of the game with relief more than elation at first; relief that we'd got a win under our belts, relief that one of the Test matches was out of the way. I imagine most people would expect me to have been absolutely over the moon at that moment, but while I was obviously very happy with the result, elation didn't hit me then. If I'd been watching in the stands it would have done, but down there on the turf, no. There was just relief to have come through after what we'd had to contend with early on in the match. I was pleased that a tactic we'd consciously adopted had worked, too.

A lot of people said after the event that the Springboks played incredibly poorly, but I'm not so sure about that. They certainly weren't playing badly at the start of the second half, but after we weathered that particular storm they tried to force the game and played right into our hands. They'd lost Lubbe, who was an influential player for them, with a hamstring problem, so they were pretty disorganised in the back line and we took full advantage of that. We toughed it out and played with a spirit that was very special indeed. Scott Gibbs, I thought, was absolutely magnificent, bullying the 'Boks in midfield and giving us a fantastic platform to build on. His attitude summed up our resolve not to be intimidated and that attitude spread right throughout the side. It would be unfair not to mention the contribution of every single Lions player on the pitch that day, along with all the squad members on the bench and in the stands. It was a truly historic win achieved by and for the whole squad.

Once the game was over, though, I didn't really have much time for celebrations straightaway, as the press were waiting to talk to me. I was anxious to play the win down, to stress that this was only a small part of the job done, that we had to go and win another Test match to clinch the series and that that would be extremely tough. The Springboks would have had their pride hurt by this defeat and if we thought that this had been a tough match, then just wait until Durban. I was very keen to keep everyone's feet on the ground and to make sure that the weight of expectation wasn't shifted from the 'Boks to ourselves.

Because I didn't get back into the changing-rooms immediately I didn't see the lads' initial reactions to the win, but once I'd got in there I knew the dressing-room was a very happy place to be, even though the atmosphere wasn't as mad as you'd probably think. The guys were obviously delighted to have won a Test match, but some of the players already had the attitude I'd had when talking to the media, realising that we'd still got a second one to go and win before we could claim a real victory. This game had obviously felt like a huge match, but now that it was won, the reality of the matter was that it meant nothing compared to the forthcoming game in Durban in a week's time.

Guys like Tim Rodber and Lawrence Dallaglio were being very sensible about things and I remember that Woody wasn't really saying much at all, sitting there absolutely knackered after the game. I think Scott Gibbs summed up the mood of the players best when he came up to me and said, 'There's no way we're going to roll over next week after this, Johnno. No way.' I liked that, because now we could say things like that with real conviction. You can talk about things all you like, but once you go out and do it, you have a real satisfaction in what you *have* achieved, not what you think you *can* achieve. There's nothing that compares with going out there and performing. If we'd lost that game at Newlands it would have been incredibly hard out in Durban the following week, so all in all Saturday 21 June was a great day. I was quietly satisfied with myself – without being smug. Before the match someone had brought a poster into the team room at the hotel which had been ripped down from a telegraph pole outside. It had a close-up picture of the Lions crest, including the flowers of the four home nations; I think it was an advert for a telephone company or some such thing. Anyway, the wording was quite bullish, something along the lines of 'Flower rearranging this Saturday at Newlands' – a pretty arrogant statement. We'd left that poster lying around for everyone to have a look at before we left for the game and I think it really did the trick as far as firing the players up was concerned. I remembered it again after the game and thought there was no way I wanted our lads to have that kind of a cocky attitude going into the second Test. We didn't need to be patting ourselves on the back, thinking that we were so great and that the job was done. The job was a very, very long way from being done.

At the after-match press conference Fran made the usual speeches, but what else can you say? It's only the first game. You can't rub it in because you can be left with egg on your face if you get too full of yourselves. It was a real concern and when we finally got back to the hotel I asked Lawrence to get up and say something about keeping things on track for another week, to think about Durban and winning the series more than the win we'd just had today. He agreed to do it, but then Fran got up himself and said all that needed to be said about attitude, so Lol didn't bother. That was that, then, and off we popped into the town for something to eat at Cantina Tequila. I saw my girlfriend Kay for the first time after the match – she'd flown in the previous day – which was great and we had a lot of fun. A lot of the former stars of England's rugby team were out on the town: Dean Richards, Mike Teague, Wade Dooley and Peter Winterbottom, who were down playing in a couple of testimonial matches, I believe. I don't really know any of them that well aside from Deano, who's with me at Leicester, but I shook hands, said hello and had a chat. I liked them. They weren't the kind of sad folk who always have to go on about how they were better rugby players in their day than anyone around now. I've got nothing but respect for what they achieved in the game, but they're not under any illusions about who or what they are – they're just great blokes and I enjoyed their company. I was talking to Teague and he said, 'We're just sad old bastards now. You're the boys,' which was great. These guys are the kind of rugby players you want to be when you retire, not some venomous, bitter bloke with a chip on your shoulder. You want to enjoy scenes like this, just like any supporters – of which there were many larging it about the place. The Lions fans had obviously enjoyed the win and were determined to make the most of their night out in Cape Town. Me? I decided to head for bed early. I was already turning my thoughts to Durban.

CHAPTER FIFTEEN

Keeping on Top of Things

To keep the spirit in the squad as strong as it had been all the way through the tour, we had decided that the victorious team from Saturday would go training with the lads preparing for Tuesday's game against the Free State Cheetahs on the Sunday morning. Gibbsy had come up with the idea on the bus on the way back to the hotel the previous night, which was a quick and easy thing to say at the time, when everybody was pumped up with the excitement of the win, but every single player turned up the following morning, which pleased me a great deal. As it happens, I think it was a good thing that we did show some solidarity with the lads, because all through training it was raining quite heavily, coming in almost horizontally, and it was crap, just a horrible day. It took the entire morning to get through the preparations the side needed for Tuesday because the weather was hindering things so much, so the lads who hadn't played in the Test probably needed a lift. Simon Shaw had flu, so I subbed in the scrum session with Tim Rodber and Jerry Davidson. My shoulder wasn't feeling too bad, which, I worked out later, was probably because I was still on a high after the Test match and the adrenaline was taking care of the pain. That would come the next day, on Monday.

We were due to leave Cape Town for Durban and after training headed back to the hotel and started to pack. It was really noticeable now how everyone in South Africa wanted to shake us by the hand. The South Africans seem to have a thing about it, which is a bit weird, but nice all the same. They all seemed to be going out of their way to say 'well done', which was a little different from what we thought. I expected some of them to be a little difficult about losing, knowing how seriously they take their rugby and how important the sport is to them.

Anyway, on to Durban. The flight was great because, naturally, I managed to sleep all the way, and when we touched down the weather was 25 degrees in the middle of winter. I have a soft spot for Durban and if there is anywhere I could call home on tour, then this is it. I'd spent time there during the '95 World Cup and England were also based there in '94. Durban's a place where you can chill out and take it easy on your body. We checked into the Holiday Inn Crowne Plaza in Durban itself, a different hotel from when we had stayed in the suburb of Umhlanga a couple of weeks back, but a good one all the same, seeing as it's right on the beach. My only concern in arriving at such a beautiful spot was that it would be very easy to slip into a holiday vibe, to lose sight of the job that we still had to do and to lose our focus. I knew that everyone would have to apply themselves to the task in hand, but I was also confident that all the squad had proved through-out the tour that they had the right mental attitude and that they wouldn't let either me or themselves down now.

Selection for Tuesday's match against the Free State Cheetahs was a predictable business, with Neil Jenkins getting the short straw for the trip up to Bloemfontein. There are 35 squad members and 21 had been involved in the Saturday match, so it's a simple question of mathe-matics to work out that someone is going to have to double up. We selected Nigel Redman as skipper, which I thought was a great choice and a really big honour for him. He's a good senior player and is comfortable speaking to the players while allowing them to have their say as well. All in all we believed he was the right man for the job.

By Monday morning I was glad that I wasn't playing on Tuesday as the stiffness from Saturday had finally set in. I needed to put a good rehab session in and I may have been a little too tough on myself, doing an hour and three-quarters in the gym followed by a two- to three-mile run around the suburb of La Lucia. It's a great place to blow the cobwebs away, a quiet area full of nice houses next to the beach.

By the time I got back to the hotel, though, things weren't quite so peaceful. Suddenly the place was full of secretaries who were in town for some kind of conference. They were a noisy bunch and when I bumped into them I have to say it was the first time in my life that I've suffered from sexual harassment. It was exactly the same as a pretty girl walking past a group of lairy blokes on a building site. There were a few of us walking downstairs in our tracksuits and these women were all hanging about. I suppose they were in their late thirties, and at that age they really don't mind saying exactly what's on their minds. They were giggling, saying, 'Ooh, you look like big, strong lads' and a few other things which I'm too embarrassed to go into here. They were giving it the works, which I thought was quite funny, a good laugh. The hotel was really buzzing that day. It was very full and there were loads of distractions . . . besides the secretaries! The Harlem Globetrotters were also staying there, and with the overall feel of the place, I think I was starting to get paranoid about everyone's eye being taken off the ball. Saturday was all-important.

The team from last Saturday had an early session on Tuesday morning involving lots of scrummaging. My shoulders were killing me after the general battering they had taken in the Test match and the hot and muggy weather made training even more unpleasant. The ground where we were practising, Durban High School Old Boys' ground, is in a natural dip, which makes the air very still. It's just the worst place to go and work, with absolutely no breeze. When you're feeling tired it makes things doubly difficult, and once the session started it was very noticeable that people were struggling to get going. Jim Telfer was giving everybody grief, getting a little too frantic, if you ask me, and my ears were getting cut to ribbons while we were scrummaging. I was a bit pissed off, to be frank. The only problem I ever had with Jim on the tour was that when he gets very enthusiastic about things he's got to do everything at a million miles an hour. Sometimes he thinks everything's got to be really frantic in order to be intense. Now, I believe you can be intense, you can do things right and you can do them aggressively without having to get wild about it. I think you have to be careful with certain players, particularly the Irish lads. You need rugby players to be thinking sharp, and rushing around like headless chickens isn't always the best way to give them that clarity of thought. It can make people a little bit panicky and I thought I'd seen some of that in our play too. I thought we'd occasionally made mistakes by being overeager. You need to go out to play matches and be intense without being frantic, and you need to be cool and calm. The fact that I was hurting as well didn't help my mood any.

I had a little word with Jim, and tried to calm him down, but he'd

be going, 'Right, right. We'll have some water now! Right. Quick! Run
. . . run and get your water. Over here, we'll do this now.' It wasn't a
major thing, but we needed a sense of perspective. I could feel that the
way the session was going we'd end up in the realms of 'Just one more,
just one more, just one more', and everyone's heard that far too many
times. 'One more' means seven more. When people say 'We'll go out
and do 24 scrums', then you'll end up going out and doing 24 scrums
plus another six. At the time, running up and down in the humidity
and with bodies hurting, it probably wasn't the most sensible thing to
do.

After we'd finished this gruelling workout I got back to the hotel to
see off to Bloemfontein the lads playing against Free State Cheetahs.
They'd chartered a flight from Durban to get them there and were
going to come back the same night rather than stay over, which was an
unusual way of doing things, but nobody seemed particularly unhappy
about the arrangements. Geech had picked up some kind of a virus, so
he didn't make the trip at all.

Once I'd seen the lads off I met up with Will Carling, who'd just
turned up. The atmosphere was a bit weird because apparently he'd
made some comments in the press about the Lions and how he didn't
see how the whole idea of it could possibly survive in the modern,
professional era. Fran had taken exception to what Will had said and
didn't want him around, but I didn't think Will was being particularly
poisonous. He was just telling it as he saw it in the professional world.
I think Fran blanked him, though. He said to one of the lads, 'What's
he doing here? *He* doesn't like the Lions,' but the way I saw it, Will was
just over for a couple of days and felt like having a bit of a chat. He
wasn't getting in the way at all, so a few of us had lunch with him,
which was fine.

Andy Keast took a video session in the afternoon and then we
settled down to watch the match in the evening, a 7.15 p.m. kick-off.
Or at least we tried to . . . We had a big screen hooked up to a TV in
the team room. We needed to record the match to study afterwards, so
we hooked up the video to record, then found that we didn't have
enough leads to actually watch the match at the same time. We ended
up missing the first five minutes of the game while people scrambled
around looking for more leads. People were going ballistic and everyone in the hotel got abused to death by the players.

Once we finally got hooked up it was great to watch the boys. They turned in a superb performance, one of the best on the tour, especially after a lot of people had been saying that the Free State were one of the strongest provincial sides in South Africa. They'd been tipped to win the domestic Currie Cup, but we just steamrollered in and absolutely blew them away. Eric Miller was superb, Backy was brilliant, Catty played well. The whole side showed what great rugby the Lions could play, demonstrating the flowing moves which, to my mind, are what the game's all about. Everything was looking great, we were winning 31–13, and we were really enjoying the performance until Will Greenwood got concussed just before half-time. At first we didn't think it was that bad, but on the replay you could see that he'd been pulled around quite quickly, then slammed into the ground as his head shot backwards. It wasn't very nice.

We knew it was a bad injury because Will was completely motionless, then his legs started twitching and convulsing. The players on the pitch all gathered round him straightaway and it was one of those times when you thank God that you've got a good medical team. In situations like that, if you've got some jobsworth who doesn't really know what he's doing, there's a chance that some really serious damage will be done. Luckily our doctor James Robson and physio Mark Davies were on the pitch in a flash and realised how serious the problem was. Their quick thinking and expert diagnosis averted what could have been a far more serious problem. Will was in a rotten way, suffering from bad concussion. He had a bit of a fit, too, which the television didn't talk about, probably because they didn't know what was going on. We only found out afterwards ourselves. Often there's no real explanation as to why someone will react that violently to a sudden belt on the head; it just happens because some people are naturally more sensitive. The worst thing about the whole incident was that I assumed that Will's girlfriend was at home watching the match, not knowing how he was. We all had mobile phones with us and were frantically trying to get in touch with Bloemfontein to find out if Will was all right so that we could phone his girlfriend and reassure her. Eventually we got a phone call back from the game saying that he was okay, and when he finally came round in the hospital he phoned her himself, just to confirm to her that there was no permanent damage. Typically, we found out later that his girlfriend hadn't been watching the match at all and was blissfully unaware of all the high drama that was going on – which was probably for the best, in retrospect.

Once we knew that Will was okay, we turned our attentions back to the match. I was delighted with the way we played, running in seven tries and playing with a style that was a joy to watch. Fran said afterwards that to go and play at altitude against one of the top Super-12 teams in a midweek fixture and to produce that kind of rugby was absolutely outstanding, and he was dead right. He said how proud he was of them, and so was I. Bentos had run in three tries, staking a real claim for a Test place, and Stimmo had knocked four conversions and three penalties over, both great individual performances. The next morning's selection for the second Test was going to be a real headache again, but it was a good problem to have to deal with all the same.

Wednesday's training session was put back to the afternoon to allow the boys who flew back late from Bloemfontein the chance to catch up on some much-needed rest. Will Greenwood had been kept in hospital overnight for observation and arrived back in Durban at lunchtime, although there was no question of him being able to play in any more matches on the tour. To be honest, he looked a bit of a mess and had done his shoulder in as well as suffering from concussion. I know that it can sometimes take a player quite a while to get his confidence back after a particularly nasty injury, but hoped that wouldn't be the case with Will. It was a shame for him because his form had been quite outstanding and his claims for a Test place would have been very hard to ignore.

The selection meeting for the second Test in the morning proved to be a tough one, the hardest position to call being winger. We were undecided about whether to play Ieuan Evans again or give Bentos a chance and there was also the back-row combination to agree on. Geech was very undecided who to go for, John or Ieuan, and it was a very close call, but in the end we went for Ieuan. It's all too easy to name the same team that has won the last game for you without even really thinking through the differences that you might encounter in the next match, and we didn't want to get caught in that trap, so we decided that we'd put Eric Miller and Neil Back on the bench to give us the option to change things around quite considerably if we needed to. We decided that we wouldn't announce the side until Thursday, however, to keep squad spirit high and to keep the Springboks guessing.

Of course, the best-laid plans are often prone to go awry, and during the afternoon session Ieuan went down with a pulled groin which put him out of the rest of the tour. It was tragic to see a great player like Ieuan bow out in this way and the whole session was definitely affected for the worse by his breaking down. Then, as if that wasn't bad enough, later in the session Jerry Davidson went down and was taken off for X-rays. We really thought he'd broken his leg. You get used to injuries in rugby and if you see a guy go down you can usually tell almost at once how bad the injury is. We all thought it was bad enough to mean that Jerry would be out of the tour. He was a very popular member of the squad, too, so it affected morale all round. Then Tom Smith started holding his neck again after a maul. People were dropping like flies, so we called a quick halt to proceedings. We really didn't need these kinds of things happening three days before one of the most important matches of our lives.

A blessed relief! It turned out after X-rays that Jerry's injury was by no means as bad as we'd feared, which meant that the mood was considerably perkier when we returned to training in the early evening to do line-out work. It was a good session, too, except that the press had announced that we'd be training and huge crowds of kids turned out to watch us. We signed hundreds of autographs after we'd finished, but the queues of people waiting didn't seem to be getting any smaller, a bit like the shopping-mall experience. In the end we had to cut things short and shoot off, otherwise we would have been there all night.

With Ieuan and Will Greenwood now out of the tour we decided that we would need cover for the one provincial match against Northern Free State towards the end of the tour. It wouldn't make sense flying someone all the way from the UK, but there was a perfect solution. Tony Stanger was on tour in South Africa with Scotland A, so he could hook up with us for the one game and not cause too much disruption to anyone.

I was persuaded to go and watch the Harlem Globetrotters in the evening. I wasn't really convinced by the idea, but was dragged along in time for the second half, only to find that it wasn't much of a spectacle after all. I just sat there quietly munching my popcorn. At one time the Globetrotters were the most well-known sports team in the world, but for whatever reason the shine seems to have worn off and I was glad to leave. It seemed like a far better idea to end the night by going for a Chinese with my agent Darren Grewcock, who was still hanging around enjoying himself, and Richard the masseur.

The Test team was announced on Thursday morning and read as follows:

Jenkins, Bentley, Gibbs, Guscott, Tait, Townsend, Dawson, Smith, Wood, Wallace, Johnson, Davidson, Dallaglio, Rodber, Hill.

The news that John Bentley was in the starting line-up had really aroused the interest of the press, and the snappers were all over him. I was pleased for Bentos and hoped things went well for him in the game. In many ways he'd come to symbolise a lot of the bulldog spirit, grit and determination of the touring party. He had scored the try of the series against Gauteng, had had a bit of a running battle with the South African winger James Small in the game against Western Province and had built up a real rapport with all the Lions supporters. He had real personality on the field – and off it too, for that matter. He was always the joker, always bubbly, and whether it was shouting at people in training or nicking Bob Burrows's seat, there was never a dull moment with Bentos around. Knowing the kind of character he was, I also knew that if he didn't perform against the Springboks, if he had a bad game, it wouldn't have been like any other person having an off-day. It would have meant more to him than simply not playing particularly well. A bad game in the Lions jersey he had fought so hard to win would really hurt his pride.

I had the usual round of interviews for press and TV to contend with, although sadly there was no Miss South Africa with her inane questions. It wasn't too bad this time. After all, there are worse places to talk to the press than poolside in the blazing sun of Durban. I even got to go to the beach again for more photos, where the number of Lions supporters hanging about now was quite incredible. Obviously the win in Cape Town had really got everybody up for it and the mood of the supporters seemed very upbeat. They were convinced we could pull off another win.

The team meeting was held in the early evening and Geech spent 45 minutes discussing how the Springboks would play with the new players they'd brought in like Montgomery and van Schalkwyk. To be fair, we actually picked up on how they were going to play straight off, really, which wasn't particularly difficult. We knew that with Lubbe and Mulder out injured they'd have to change their tactics. They'd kick more and drive at us through the forwards, which meant that we really needed to hold on to the ball more.

The evening was rounded off with a visit to Langoustines, one of my favourite restaurants in South Africa. It was nice to get out of the hotel; they drive you a bit crazy after a while, what with the food always being the same, either chicken or beef . . . and hotels in South Africa can't make a sandwich to save their lives!

The mood at the restaurant was very buoyant. Eric Miller and Backy, in particular, were delighted to have made the bench and Backy really got into another round of 'Guess who's coming to dinner'. Whatever turns you on, as they say . . .

The day before the Test was a much-needed rest day. A couple of friends of mine who were in Durban popped by to visit and after a spot of lunch we headed off to the beach. It seemed like the whole of Britain and Ireland had ended up on this one strip of beach and everyone was having a whale of a time. The prospect of sunbathing and swimming in the clear, blue, warm water was very appealing, but I knew it was vital to stay out of the sun so that the heat didn't knacker me out.

Geech's traditional pre-match trip this time was to a local bird park, which gave the lads another great opportunity to have a moan, but I actually thought it was a pretty good outing. They put on a little bird show for us. If you put out your hand the birds would fly on to it, or they would swap perches or walk in and out of bird cages. It was pretty unusual but fairly entertaining and, again, it was good for us all to be together, focusing on the match. The evening meeting was brought forward and again felt like a good one to me, full of confident talk and positive input. There wasn't anything much for me to say. I felt that everyone had shown the attitude that was expected of them and everyone knew exactly what they had to do the following day. All through the tour I never felt that I needed to do any kind of rabble-rousing about the pride that needed to be shown in wearing the Lions shirt. They all knew that anyway. I hadn't had any disciplinary or attitude problems throughout the tour, so why would it start now? I thought it was better to let everyone relax their minds and prepare however they saw fit. I opted to go to the cinema to see Steven

Spielberg's follow-up to *Jurassic Park*, *The Lost World*. It was all right. I'd probably take Kay to watch it, but I doubt I'd go on my own. Which is about the limit of my film-critic abilities. I think I'll stick to rugby . . .

CHAPTER SIXTEEN

Winners

Saturday morning. This was it: the moment of truth. We all knew this was the match that could make the 1997 Lions squad to South Africa legendary. If we could perform the way we'd done in Cape Town the week before, we were convinced we could do it. Jim Telfer gave us a great motivational speech before the match. He told us to visualise what we were going to do on the pitch, the big hits we were going to make, the something we'd come up with that was going to be that little bit special. I visualised a big score, winning a big line-out. People were all seeing themselves making big tackles and kicks, but what I thought was particularly good about this session was that nobody was going through the motions. Everyone really committed themselves to the cause at that point. There was no turning back. We said we were going to do it so that was it, we were going to do it. No problem.

If anything, the atmosphere in Durban for the second Test was even more electric than it had been a week earlier in Cape Town. It seemed like there were almost as many Lions fans crammed into King's Park as there were Springboks supporters, and I could feel their expectations bearing down on us from the terraces. We knew that the one thing we couldn't do was allow the opposition to swarm all over us the way they had at Newlands, but, to be honest, right from the off we found ourselves on the back foot again. We kicked off, the ball fell straight to the 'Boks and they ran all over us, like a runaway rhino. They were awarded two penalties in the first six minutes, which Henry Honiball missed, and again we took our chances when they came our way. It was a similar sort of game to that in Cape Town; they started off well and had opportunities to score with the boot but didn't take them, whereas we did. They scored three tries and we didn't score any. Fair enough, van der Westhuizen squirmed through for a try after we took a dummy, no problem. But on Montgomery's try we passed the ball to them, and we then failed to make a tackle when Joubert went in at the corner for their third. I'm sure if they had passed the ball to us like that then we could have scored tries too. And even after Joubert had scored that third try in the first part of the second half, the score was only 15–9. A try and a conversion and we would have been right back in the game.

We had to dig deep, no doubt about it, but they gave away silly penalties again, which they should have known we were going to score. People say that if they hadn't wasted all their penalties then they would have walked away with the game, but you just can't say that with the benefit of hindsight. If they'd kicked a penalty and scored each time, we'd then have kicked off from the halfway line deep into their territory and things could have been different; we would have been back and pressing them. When they missed a penalty, we dropped out from the twenty-two so they got the ball straight back and, perhaps, had another shot at us. If they'd put points on the board it may have spurred us on to greater things. Who's to know? But, admittedly, if they'd kicked 21 points then of course it would have been a lot harder for us to come through. It wasn't all one-way traffic, though. When Gibbsy started getting the ball and running at them he was giving them problems, and I remember one line-out where we put the ball wide to Alan Tait and he got round his man and was off up the wing.

We had our chances and it was one of those games where you had to keep calling upon all your reserves of energy, physical and mental, and keep believing that you could do it, that you could win. As long as the Springboks were giving away silly penalties I always thought we had a chance, and Jenks was magnificent again. How he stays so ice-cool under such intense pressure is beyond me, but he kicked two great penalties in the second half – which made it five out of five – to drag us back level, and I was immensely proud of him. I thought that if things stayed the way they were, at 15–15, then at the very least we couldn't lose the series. But then, of course, came the magical moment. To be honest, I couldn't believe it when Jerry struck the ball and sent it soaring through the posts for the winning drop goal. I thought we were a lot further out when he shot it over, but we were actually pretty close. I don't remember very much about the build-up, only that

Gregor was driving for the line – I think he was going left – and the ball was recycled very quickly for Jerry. As soon as the ball went out to him I thought he was going to do it. There was no one else wide, so there was no other option. I was thinking to myself, 'You're there, the posts are right in front of you. Just knock it over.' And that's just what he did.

It was a fantastic sight to see the ball sail between the posts and I think a few of the lads had a bit of a crazy moment, because they knew that we were so close to what we'd worked so hard for, but I just wheeled away and started running back straightaway. Why? Because I thought I was about to experience the longest five minutes of my life. In many ways it *was* the longest five minutes of my life, but I was glad that I was down there on the field playing. If I'd been up in the stands watching I don't think I could have coped with the tension. I feel sorry for all the Lions fans who had to go through it, because it must have been absolute agony. I'd have been biting my nails down to my elbows. On the field I felt fairly in control – apart from one occasion when the Springboks, mounting desperate attacks to claw their way back into the game, kicked through while I was already on the floor. I looked back, thinking, 'I can't see who's going to get that first. Please, Christ, let it be us.' Thank God we did get there, but I didn't actually see who it was. Austin Healey saved one on the ground really near to our own line that was dangerous too, but we all tackled exceptionally well in that last period.

There was one moment when there was a loose ruck towards the end of the game where the Springboks had control of the ball. I remember van der Westhuizen slowly putting his hands on the ball and looking at his options. I could have just raced through and grabbed it, and it would have been 50-50 that I'd get penalised. I just thought, 'Look, you can have the ball there. If you drop a goal, we get a draw, and if you score a try then that's just our tough luck, but I'm not going to give a penalty away and put three points on a plate for you.' The move came to nothing. We fought tremendously hard throughout that last period of the game, kept tackling them and knocking them back and then when the whistle finally went . . . well, it didn't sink in straightaway. We were all a little bit stunned that we'd done it, that we'd actually managed to do what we'd all worked so hard to achieve. A Test series win against South Africa in their own back yard. Then we just went bananas.

I wasn't really aware of what was going on all around me in the stadium, I was only aware of the lads on the pitch. There weren't any tears, just relief and delight that we'd pulled off another victory. It was great. Geech came on, Fran came on, all the rest of the lads. It was one of those times when you think to yourself, 'Christ, you've got to savour this moment because you'll never experience anything like this ever again.' That's what I was trying to do at the time, but it was difficult. To be honest, I look back on the aftermath of the match out on the pitch and I can't really remember that much about it.

I suppose I could have watched the scenes on video, but I haven't even watched the match on tape. I don't know why, really. I just haven't got round to it, I suppose. I probably will at some point. I wouldn't be surprised if some people think that's a bit of a weird attitude, but that's just the way I am. We've won the series. I know we've won the series and I don't feel a desperate urge to relive it all. When you're on tour you're still living it, it's happening right there and then, and you can't match that feeling of experiencing something momentous. When you get home you just want to go, 'Well, I'm home now,' and that special moment's gone for the time being. If somebody put the video on right now I'd probably watch it, but I wouldn't go out of my way to do so. Maybe I'd go through the video looking at the technical points of the game. But that doesn't mean I wasn't emotional about what happened. Anyone who saw the interview I gave on Sky television the minute we came off the pitch will know that's not true. I was very emotional, almost in tears, and I was glad that I used that opportunity to give credit to the players who had had to go back home injured: Doddie Weir, Rob Howley, Scott Quinnell, Paul Grayson. The Test series victory really was for them just as much as for any of the players who were out there when we finally clinched things. I definitely got a bit choked when I was talking about the guys. I was just a little bit stunned that it had all happened the way I'd always dreamed it would. We had known we were only 80 minutes away from glory at the start of the match, but we never really let ourselves dare to think about it.

When I finally got off the pitch after celebrating the win, it seemed that I had a million and one things to do at once. I did all the press interviews, then had to go for a urine test before getting changed and finally going upstairs to do the speeches. When I was showering in the dressing-room, all the boys had got their shirts unbuttoned and they all had their collars sticking out for miles, a sort of '70s look. Taity looked particularly fetching with a pair of massive shades on too, but I didn't think it would be appropriate for me to go up to do the speeches looking like a member of the Jackson Five. Joel Stransky, the great South African fly-half who's my team-mate at Leicester and good friends with plenty of the boys, came in and said, 'Well done, you bastards,' which was good of him, but it was hard not to gloat over the victory.

Once we were all done with official duties, we headed back to the hotel and had a few drinks in the team room, just the squad together. To be truthful, yet again the atmosphere probably wasn't as jubilant as people might have expected, because I still don't think it had really sunk in. We were still thinking of the victory today as just another big win. Well, that's not strictly true, I suppose. Obviously people had appreciated what had happened, but we didn't really know exactly what we should be doing. We sat around and had a few beers and I guess there was a bit of champagne there, but what do you do when you get back to the hotel after a day like that? What do you do when you've won a Test series? It was simply a case of 'We've won the series, thanks for coming. See ya.'

Most of the guys decided they wanted to go to TJ's, where a lot of the Lions supporters would have gathered to celebrate, but the thought of so many people the worse for wear with drink and going absolutely ballistic didn't really appeal to me. Kay was still out in South Africa and I knew my dad was supposed to be staying at the Royal Hotel in Durban, so I thought we'd both go down there to say hello to him, although by the time we got there, about 10 o'clock, he'd already gone to bed. He'd had a very long day, if you know what I mean, so I just hooked up with a few of my mates for a couple of beers. It might not have been everybody's idea of how to celebrate a Lions series victory, but I was perfectly happy and had a good night. Everybody was just extremely happy. I did some steady drinking but nothing too out-rageous, and I never drink shorts, which probably helps to keep me on an even keel. I must have knocked a few back, though, because I didn't get to bed until something like three in the morning, although God knows what time the rest of the lads must have got in – and in what state. I know that a few of the boys – Backy, Tom Smith and some others – came back to the hotel very late and then went straight down to the beach to watch the sun come up. Tom walked out of the hotel with the duvet from his room wrapped around his shoulders and they took a load of beer down with them. Naturally everyone ended up crashing out on the beach with just their heads poking up out of the duvet – and, strangely enough, while they were asleep somebody came along and nicked all their booze. Well, you would, wouldn't you?

CHAPTER SEVENTEEN

The Comedown

The following day I woke up mid-morning and dragged myself downstairs with the intention of going to the beach. There was an optional trip to the gym lined up, but I was in no fit state to contemplate that and I thought that I'd earned myself some relaxation time, so the beach won out. I sat there in my swimming trunks and T-shirt with Gibbsy, Woody, Austin Healey and our physio, Mark Davies, just taking the whole thing in. The one thought that popped into my mind? Nothing much deeper than 'happy days'. For some reason it was a bit overcast, but nothing could cloud my mood that morning. I wanted to soak in the feeling of having pulled off the series win. I wanted to enjoy thinking about all the people who had written us off and about all the hard work that every single man on the tour had put in.

I had a good 20-minute swim in the sea, which was very enjoyable, then decided that I was hungry and wanted something to eat. Woody, Austin and I went off to a beachfront place called Joe Cool's and ordered up burgers, which were very tasty. There was only one problem. We suddenly realised that not one of us had a penny to pay for anything. We'd all walked down to the beach in our trunks and no one was carrying any cash. This seemed a fine state to be in. Here we were, the most famous rugby team in the world on that particular day, and not one of us could afford to pay for a poxy burger! Unfortunately, the restaurant's manageress didn't see the funny side of things either and was less than impressed when we said one of us would have to run back to the hotel to get some money to pay the bill. She was very serious and said, 'Now listen, boys. I'll trust you to pay me the money, but you must know that if you don't come back, wherever you may go I'll find you and I'll screw you up, believe me!' I decided that the safest option was to go back with the cash before I left for Johannesburg that day on the last internal flight of the tour. Judging by the look on her face I have no doubt that if I'd tried to do a runner she would have been as good as her word. And how difficult would it have been to find a six foot seven British Lions captain anyway?!

We checked out of the Crowne Plaza at 12.30 p.m. and were given a standing ovation by all the supporters who were milling about in the hotel lobby, which was both nice and embarrassing at one and the same time. Mark Davies certainly enjoyed the moment, though, walking on to the team bus and opening his arms wide with a great flourish to take the applause as if it was meant for him and him alone – a very funny moment. All the cleaners and maids at the hotel also gave us a very nice send-off, singing and dancing in the traditional African style, which was very impressive. Mind you, even the tap-dancing jazz band would have met with my approval on that day, given the good mood I was in.

On the bus I felt particularly tired after yesterday's exertions and was very much looking forward to our next destination, the Riverside Sun in Vanderbijlpark, a small town about 90 minutes away from Johannesburg. The idea was that we'd have four days' rest and recuperation there because we'd all be knackered, giving the guys a great opportunity to recharge their batteries. I thought it sounded like a great idea . . . until we arrived there, that is. The Riverside Sun was a rather optimistic name for the hotel. The weather was absolutely freezing, which would have been bad enough in itself, but having just left the sunny, warm beaches of Durban, the shock to the system was even harder to cope with. There's no other way of describing the place except to say that it felt like an open prison. There was absolutely nothing to do, stuck in a small town in the Northern Free State or Southern Transvaal, wherever it was, and it was too cold to be outside enjoying ourselves. Fran tried to cheer us up by saying we'd have a few barbies there, but it was obviously too cold, and besides, it gets dark down there about five or six o'clock. The whole thing was just hopeless.

When we arrived at Vanderbijlpark it was the first time on the whole tour that there had been any difficulty with organisation or attitude. We now knew we'd won the series, but what we didn't know was how best to approach this last week. How should we play it? What should we do? Then we turned up at a place which was, not to put too fine a point on it, awful, and it made matters doubly difficult. We tried to organise activities, and if the weather had been nicer we'd have gone on the river and done some water sports, but it was simply too cold to contemplate. It was too late to try and find alternative accommodation and, besides, we had a game to play on the Tuesday at Welkom against Northern Free State. The management and I had a meeting on our first evening there with Tim, Lol and Jason and talked about what our goals for the last week of the tour should be. Fran and Geech were adamant that we should go out there, try to win the series 3–0 and try to play some of the free-flowing rugby that we'd produced so well in the provincial games. We were very aware that we hadn't shown that side of the Lions game in the previous two Test matches, but that's because Test matches are different; there's more pressure and you often can't physically play that kind of game and still win the match. It was a tough meeting and there was no denying that we knew it would be very difficult to get the boys up for the last Test. We could say the same things and do the same things, but human nature dictates that you will never quite be able to get the same attitude out of people once the pressure's off. It was going to be a tricky week, no doubt about it.

Selection for Tuesday's match was taken care of in the same meeting with the senior players. This time Jerry Guscott got the short straw and would be asked to sit on the bench, which pleased Jason Leonard no end. He was particularly looking forward to seeing Jerry's face when the team was read out the following day, so at least one member of the party went to bed happy.

Overnight I decided that I'd have to stand up in front of the squad and tell them just how I thought we should go about the week, so at nine o'clock on Monday morning I addressed the lads to try to get them to buy into the idea of finishing the series with a bang and not a whimper. I said that I accepted that we could all relax a bit more now, but that we owed it to ourselves to finish off the series on a high and to play to the best of our abilities, starting with the game against Northern Free State on Tuesday. To show some solidarity in the camp it was agreed that everyone would travel to Welkom for the game, despite it being a fairly long journey. I asked Jerry Guscott what he thought of my ideas and unfortunately this time I got the wrong answer. Jerry's opinion was that we should just relax and take it easy for the week, and while I thought that he personally could probably get away without putting too much hard yakka in and still play well in a game of rugby, I believed that most of the players still needed to train hard and that the forwards in particular needed to keep their intensity levels up. Maybe I shouldn't have asked him.

I looked to Lol for a bit of support, which he immediately gave me, saying, 'No. I think we should keep going and we should go out there and beat the 'Boks 3–0.' I appreciated his comments, but I think it takes one hell of a speech to change people's opinions if they've really made their minds up about how they're going to approach things. If we'd gone out to South Africa as favourites to win and were only 2–0 up, then I think we could have said, 'Look, we've won it, but we've not been good enough.' But if you go out there as supposed no-hopers and you've already achieved more than anyone expected you to and have only lost one game on tour, it's very difficult not to think, 'We've done it.' We had done it to a certain degree, but we could have done more. Maybe Monday morning was the wrong time to have had the meeting, I don't know. Maybe we should have done it later in the week. Whatever, I didn't feel that it was a particularly successful get-together and in the end I was glad to get out for a run in Vanderbijlpark with Richard, the masseur. I think we saw about four people.

I found that I had a lot of distractions in that last week, little things that had to be sorted. For a start, there was about 35,000 rand in the kitty and we had to decide what to do with it. Should we get the managers presents? In addition everyone started to get shirts and balls out to be signed, and various other little bits and pieces cropped up. None of these things were major distractions, but they were going to get in the way of preparations and didn't help improve the generally downbeat mood.

The team for Tuesday's game in Welkom was announced and Jason Leonard couldn't stop giggling when Jerry's name was read out, although to be fair to Jerry he took the news well. The thought of a midweek game really didn't seem to inspire anyone, so to take everybody's minds off the general malaise we decided to go go-karting in the afternoon, which was good fun. I was quite surprised to see that although we were away from the main contingent of supporters, there were still plenty of autographs to sign, as well as the usual number of press interviews. The trouble was that it was almost impossible not to feel like you were going back to work on a Monday morning after spending a long and enjoyable weekend away. Bed was a welcome relief after the stress of the day, so I took the opportunity of getting my head down early. I'd had better times of it on this tour for sure.

I decided to spend the following morning going shooting. There was a Scottish guy at the hotel who told us he could organise some shooting practice for us, and both Gibbsy and I had been keen . . . at least until the morning when Gibbsy couldn't get out of bed. I ended up going with Richard Hill and once we were on the road with this fellow he started telling all sorts of grisly tales about his time in the army which I didn't really want to listen to, so it was a welcome relief finally to arrive at the range. I shot using .44s, .357s and 9mm handguns as well as an automatic rifle. It was fun, but it's never far from your mind what these weapons can do to a human body and I'm aware how sensitive some people are about the issue. I realise that you have to be very, very careful when you handle guns, and as soon as anyone sees bullets being fired from them there's no doubt about their power. I won't deny that firing guns gives you a good buzz, but only if you respect them and treat them properly.

I returned to the hotel in time to make the non-players' bus for the two-hour trip up to Welkom and today's game against Northern Free State. The players had already left at about 9.30 a.m. It was only during that journey, I think, that what we had achieved really began to sink in, and I could begin to appreciate it. For the first time on the entire tour I felt genuinely relaxed.

The North West Stadium was the smallest ground we'd visited – the Lions had never played there before – and we arrived dead on kick-off. We rushed in only to find that our seats were directly behind one of the TV cameramen, which meant that as soon as he started moving the camera to film, our view was almost entirely obscured. We decided to move to a big, grassy bank behind one set of posts so that we could actually see what was going on, but this turned out not to be the greatest idea in the world. We were all wearing our Lions tracksuits (rather than the traditional blazer and slacks, a special concession), which meant we were instantly recognisable, so I spent most of the game lying on the grass getting hassled by Afrikaners. I don't think they're deliberately trying to be rude, but I often find their manner very aggressive and 'in your face', and not really to my taste. I didn't feel like talking that day, especially when some bloke came up to me and said, 'Look, I'm nearly as tall as you' about 50 times. What do you say to someone like that? I wish I had the answer.

The game, it must be said, was something of a let-down, the only match on tour where we didn't really do ourselves justice. Fran was very unhappy with the hardness of the pitch, not to mention some dubious play from our hosts and a referee who didn't seem to have much of a grip on things. We ran in ten tries and notched up our highest points total of the tour in winning 67–39, but we also conceded more points than in any other game the Lions had played. It wasn't a match to write home about and everybody was glad to get out of the place, on the whole in one piece, although captain for the day Jason Leonard missed the whole of the second half with a thigh injury and Ronnie Regan and Kyran Bracken both took minor knocks.

We were never in danger of losing the game, but conceding so many points was disappointing. I wondered whether the whole atmosphere at Vanderbijlpark hadn't had a negative effect. It probably did; we could have scored 90 or 100 points if we'd been as good as we'd been in the previous midweek game against Free State Cheetahs, and we were slack in letting them run in so many tries. Losing Kyran and Jason had unsettled the balance of the team, but it was probably the least satisfying game on the tour as far as I was concerned, and I wasn't sorry to see the back of Welkom.

CHAPTER EIGHTEEN

Taking Over at Ellis Park

Selection for the third Test match took place on the Tuesday night when we got back to the hotel at Vanderbijlpark around nine o'clock. I was convinced that everyone would be in favour of rubber-stamping the same team from last week's winning game in Durban, but Geech was disappointed in the way the backs had performed at King's Park, particularly in the attacking side of their game. He felt they hadn't done enough. 'If you don't take the opportunity to attack whenever you can, then you're going to be under constant pressure,' he told me. 'I'm looking for the side to play the best rugby of all three Test matches on Saturday.' To that end, Geech was thinking about playing Jerry on the wing and Allan Bateman in the centre, trying to use our most naturally gifted rugby players to keep the ball moving, although, as it turned out, the injury situation meant that the plan eventually had to be abandoned.

It was a long selection meeting, with a lot of honest chat and some criticisms. I think Geech decided that he didn't want to just go through the motions by picking the same side as last week, which is why Neil Back was brought in at the expense of Richard Hill. It was hard on Hilly to have been a member of two winning Test sides and then not to be included for the third, but Geech reasoned that it would make the 'Boks think about our side and tactics a bit more, which was true. Nevertheless, I did feel a bit sorry for Richard, even though there wasn't much I could do to make him feel better.

The Test team would line up as follows:

Jenkins, Bentley, Gibbs, Guscott, Underwood, Catt, Dawson, Smith,

Regan, Wallace, Johnson, Davidson, Wainwright, Dallaglio, Back.

The Wednesday morning session was supposed to be light, but for some reason it turned out to be two hours of gruelling physical work. It was very brutal for the guys who weren't going to be part of the 21 for the Test match, but they all took a full part in proceedings, which I thought summed up the attitude of the players to a tee. Plenty of the lads were most likely hurting by now, carrying various injuries, and the last thing they really would have wanted was to pound themselves into the ground in the middle of nowhere, but, to give them their due, they all got stuck in for the good of the squad.

The afternoon session, unfortunately, proved to be a bridge too far. It was the first session that I could remember on the entire tour where people started getting on each other's backs. I detected that things were starting to go a little bit flat. Everyone wanted to get the last Test played and people were getting ratty when the ball went to ground or when someone cocked up a move. Mark Regan had finally made the side for Saturday and we had to work very hard on the line-outs, trying to get him into the swing of things, which didn't help either. There were no out-and-out slanging matches, but Geech wisely opted to cut the session short. I thought it might help if I said a few words and got the boys together. I told them that there were too many mistakes in the session, but the very fact that everyone was getting pissed off about it showed that they still really cared, which was a good thing. I said it was vital that we tried to end the tour on a positive note rather than letting things slide downhill. It was obvious that we had some psychological problems getting ourselves fired up again after the high of last Saturday, and we were struggling to get through. That was only natural. If the last match was going to be a series decider there would have been no problem. It was simply down to human nature.

We finally headed out of the Riverside Sun hotel and transferred to the Holiday Inn Crowne Plaza in Sandton to prepare ourselves for the match on Saturday. There's no need to labour the point, but let's just say that no one was shedding any tears about leaving Vanderbijlpark. Even the dreaded kit-signing session, which had been lurking in the back of my mind for a while now and was the first thing we did once we'd arrived at our new hotel, didn't seem so bad after all. Stan Bagshaw doled out all the shirts that were left over between the players and everyone sat in the team room signing shirts and balls for everyone else in the squad. I must have done something close to 500 items, which was hard going, believe me!

We also talked about what we should do with the money that had accumulated in the players' kitty from TV appearances, interview fees and such like. Of course, the first suggestion was to stick it behind the bar after the last match, which was pretty stupid when you think about it – we'd still be there now trying to drink 35,000 rands worth of lager. And anyway, with a tour sponsored by South Africa's massive beer company Lion, there was always a load of cans knocking about the place which never got drunk! Taity suggested we get a clock each, which caused even more consternation, but in the end we all agreed that we would see if we could get krugerrands for everyone. Krugerrands aren't old South African money, as I'd assumed, but quite beautiful gold coins which were still legal tender. It seemed like a good idea and an appropriate memento of South Africa, so it was decided that we would try to organise getting some picked up before we left the country.

I managed to say goodbye to Tony Stanger, who'd been called into the party when Will was injured against the Orange Free State and Icuan Evans had been forced to go home, but I was very tired again and decided to have a quiet night messing around with Hilly's Playstation. There was too much hanging about waiting for my liking now, and I couldn't wait to get to Johannesburg and get on with things.

Everyone was relieved that Thursday would be the last training session of the tour. We'd put a lot of effort into making our workouts as useful as possible and this last effort was no exception. Everyone seemed to have got over the malaise of the last few days and now seemed determined to prepare as thoroughly for the last Test as we had for the first. We worked on varying our approach to our kick-offs, because we hadn't been very effective in recovering our own kicks, but I was finding the going a bit tough; my groin was starting to play up even more and both my shoulders were sore. In all honesty, I felt like I was falling apart, and it looked like a few of the others were feeling the same way; Lol Dallaglio actually pulled up with a hamstring problem. I spoke to my surgeon Dr Gilmore and finally decided for definite that I wouldn't continue to Australia for the England match that was taking place straight after the Lions tour had finished. I'd already said that I was unavailable, but when the details for their onward journeys had been faxed over to Jason Leonard and Graham Rowntree, my name had still been on the list of players, albeit with a question mark next to it. It had half-convinced me to say that I'd go, so I'd held out some hope that I might be able to make it and have the operation a bit later. When the rest of the lads are going on to play somewhere else you naturally want to be with them, but after speaking to Gilmore and my Leicester coach Bob Dwyer I knew that wouldn't be sensible. I phoned Jack Rowell on his mobile to let him know and he was actually at Heathrow Airport, just about to board a plane for Australia. Talk about good timing!

There was a press conference organised, and the four players who'd been picked for a Test for the first time on the tour – Tony Underwood, Mike Catt, Ronnie Regan and Backy – were paraded in front of the press, which was nice for them. My mind wasn't really on the questions that were being asked as I sat there thinking about the match. I knew we were in the weakest position we'd been in before a Test, but I was still convinced we could win the game. People were saying that the chance to win the series 3–0 was as good a motivator as anything, but I wasn't at all convinced by that argument. It would have been nice, for sure, but my motivation in rugby has always been to win any game that I play in. I'm not looking at the record books to see what I've achieved and I don't really care about history. I didn't want to lose the game on Saturday purely because I didn't want the South Africans to beat us, but in my heart of hearts I knew it would be our toughest game to date. No one said it wouldn't matter if we lost, but there wasn't the same on-the-edge, do-or-die feeling. It wouldn't be the end of the world if we didn't win, no matter how much we talked about motivation and desire, and that definitely affected everyone. I knew it and I suspect that the management knew it too, although nothing was ever said to me.

The day before the big game was designated as a rest day and I decided to enjoy the free time by having a lazy lunch in Santon Square, one of the nicer spots in Jo'burg. Fran was trying to make excuses for Vanderbijlpark, saying that things would have been better if the weather had been good, but now I didn't care. I was just glad to be back in civilisation, even if it meant that I was constantly getting disturbed by excited kids looking for autographs. It was obvious that to everyone in town the Lions were now a big deal. Rugby is such a big part of the culture of South Africa that players like Joubert, Small and Kruger are sporting heroes to the white population. I suppose the fact that we'd beaten the best players their country had to offer meant that we'd gone up a lot in the estimation of the South African public.

Our afternoon outing with Geech, which had by now become part of the pre-match build-up, saw the 21 of us being shown around a local zoo. To be fair, I don't think the lads were too impressed with this little jaunt; not even when the chap who ran the place pointed out a photo of himself showing German Chancellor Helmut Kohl around. I think we were probably a bit zombie-like, which didn't make us particularly receptive to the charms of the various animals, but we were all too tired not to go along with it. We drank the fellow's tea, ate his scones, and made polite conversation, and then I left for what turned out to be an interesting meeting with the three referees who'd operated a round-robin system for the three matches, each taking two games as linesmen. Messrs Hawke, Méné and Erickson were staying at the same hotel as the Springboks and Fran, Jim, Geech and I had a fascinating time talking to them about how they'd viewed the two matches so far. We wanted to know if there was anything we were doing that they considered wrong or if they'd been happy with the way the games had been played. Some of the points they made were very thought-provoking. The Frenchman Didier Méné had penalised André Venter twice in the second Test for coming off the scrum too early, which we thought the 'Boks had been generally guilty of, and I was pleased to see that he felt the same. He'd been annoyed by the fact that he'd told them not to break off the scrum too early but they'd ignored him and carried on doing it. That kind of indiscipline had cost them valuable territory and, of course, valuable points.

We also felt that the Springboks had been very borderline on coming through offside in rucks and mauls. They were adopting a high-risk strategy, whereas we were more content to let them have the ball and rely on the strength of our tackling. We wanted to make sure the refs were aware of that, but I think they'd already noted it well enough. We knew that the South Africans had also been complaining bitterly about Paul Wallace's scrumming technique, saying that he was scrummaging illegally and wanted to find out what the refs' opinions on the matter were. Without getting too technical, as a tight head you're supposed to scrummage straight, going against two blokes at loose head and hooker. When a tight head hits as the two teams engage he will try to drop his shoulder low so that the opponents don't have an angle to push him on. Paul was scrummaging against Os du Randt, who's three stone heavier than him but who finds it hard to get low. The South Africans were getting frustrated because Paul's technique was stopping du Randt from using his natural physical superiority. The refs' opinions were that provided Paul hit the scrum straight then he would be allowed to move at an angle afterwards. On the whole we had an interesting conversation, and I was pleased to see that they were definitely human, despite what many rugby players and watchers may think of match officials!

The usual evening meeting was pretty much an open forum where people were allowed to air their views about the match and how we should approach it. Fran had to tell Tony Diprose and Rob Wainwright that their tour wasn't quite over yet and that they would have to keep off the beers because Tim Rodber had fallen ill with the flu and might be out of the Test side. Although that would unsettle the balance of the side, I was relieved that we hadn't had to deal with the problem of Tim being out a week earlier when the pressure was really on. The team needed a bit of jiggling around and it looked like Lol would move to eight and Rob would come in at six. If Scott Quinnell had been around it wouldn't have been such a problem because he takes hits the same way as Tim does, and had Eric Miller not pulled his quad running on to the field during the second Test, then things wouldn't have been so bad either. Make that a lesson to all aspiring players: always warm up properly before you come on to the field! Whatever the chopping and changing, I was glad to be going to bed with the game finally about to happen. I was tired of all the waiting.

We spent our last practice session on the morning of the match working with Rob to get him into the swing of things, and the forwards were then all a little bit surprised when we got the biggest bollocking we've ever had back in the team room at the hotel. Jim Telfer went ballistic, telling us that we hadn't been good enough in the first two Tests, that we'd always been second best to the Springboks and that we'd better get our bloody act together for today's game, otherwise we'd get slaughtered. I was a bit taken aback, even though I recognised that there was something of a tactical reason behind his outburst. Jim's so passionate that you can't simply switch off when he's ranting, and I think the rest of the lads were shell-shocked by the severity of his attack. It worried me that parts of what he was saying were true and that the lads would know that. I didn't want them to get downhearted by his stinging criticism because that would achieve the opposite effect to what we needed, to go out with a positive attitude for the last game. Maybe I was overconcerned for the rest of the boys, though, because when we got on the bus to head out to Ellis Park for the game I couldn't see anyone in tears and the general mood of the team seemed to be good.

If you can't get motivated to play at Ellis Park then you can't get motivated to play rugby anywhere. The feel of the ground is very different from most of the major stadiums in South Africa. It's set in a built-up area rather than in the suburbs where you tend to find most of the other grounds, and it is an awesome place to play in. Plenty of people consider it the home of South African rugby and I wouldn't disagree with them, although I'm sure there are folk in Cape Town and Durban who would beg to differ. Whatever, running out as captain of the Lions for the final time on the tour gave me a buzz, and I was determined to give it everything I had and to go out on a high note. My optimism didn't last too long, it must be said.

Yet again we found that we couldn't match the Springboks in the first quarter of the game. They'd had a couple of enforced changes and Joubert was injured again, but if anything this seemed to make them more determined. The 'Boks came at us with all guns blazing, determined that they weren't going to be the side that went down in history as the first ever South African team to suffer a home whitewash by the Lions. As far as we were concerned, in some ways I think we might have overemphasised our desire to play some flowing, exciting rugby in this final game. We were chucking the ball all over the place, trying to get it out wide at every opportunity and when we made mistakes there was a lot of room for the Springboks to exploit. At times we were playing good stuff and making some breaks – Tony Underwood had one jinking run that nearly got him free – but we paid the price for making mistakes and this time the South Africans punished us. They'd brought in Jannie de Beer for his first cap over Henry Honiball to try and exploit any penalty decisions that went their way. He wasn't as good a rugby player as Honiball, but he knew how to put the ball between the sticks. Of course, what people forgot was that the reason Honiball was dropped was because we'd done a great job keeping him out of the game and stopping him from putting other players through, which was his speciality. Whatever, the change worked for South Africa and within the first 15 minutes they were leading 13–0.

It was a weird game to play in. The pace was incredible, the most physically demanding of all the Tests, and the atmosphere on the pitch definitely wasn't the same as it had been. Maybe the Springboks were really feeling the pressure not to lose this game – the whole country would have been at their throats if they had – but there was a nasty element in the match, with a few cheap shots being doled out. Venter got warned when there was a big brawl, then Paul Wallace got whacked a couple of times in the scrum, probably as retribution for what they saw as illegal scrummaging. I thought it was all a bit pointless, because the 'Boks were playing well and were on top. The first two matches had been relatively clean, so it was a shame that things had degenerated.

We hauled ourselves back to 13–9 by half-time and I thought that there was still everything to play for. All the way through the tour we'd been in this kind of situation and had come back strongly towards the end of the game. We'd suffered a couple of injuries here, though; Jerry had broken his arm and Tony Underwood had had to come off, but Allan Bateman came on at centre and we put Stimmo out on the wing, which I thought gave us as good a chance of coming back as any.

We started the second half much better than the first, and we had some cracking chances which we didn't take. We'd managed to get back to a position where we were in with a realistic chance of taking the game, but for the first time in the whole tour I think we found ourselves wanting. Tiredness had more of an effect than anything, to be honest, and we simply faded away in the last 15 minutes of the game. The Springboks ran in two tries in the last five minutes and I felt that there wasn't much I could do about it. I was feeling the pace very badly, like I had nothing at all left in the tank. I was just shattered! We'd played some of our best rugby during the game, but the crucial difference between this performance and the other two Tests was that we didn't make things count at the key moments. If you don't do that at the highest level then you'll lose – and so it proved.

When the final whistle went I was actually in the middle of a fight with Dawie Theron, so my mind was a little too preoccupied to stop and take everything in. When I finally disentangled myself from Theron I started to think about things a bit. We'd lost the match but won the series, so how was I supposed to feel? I wasn't too sure. You can't come off the field having lost a game of rugby with a big smile on your face, and, anyway, I was genuinely feeling a bit down because we'd conceded two sloppy tries right at the death. The players came together for a team huddle and Bentos took control of the situation. 'We may have lost today, but we're the real winners,' he said. 'We've come down here and done what we set out to do, which we should be massively proud of, and we should share it with our fans and say goodbye to them.' It was exactly the right thing to say at that moment and I think all the players realised that what we'd done really was something immense, something that every single player in the squad had worked his heart out for, and we owed it to ourselves to savour the last moments of the tour on the field together.

It seemed to take an eternity for the officials to get themselves sorted to present us with the series trophy. The South African fans were leaving the ground in droves and it must have taken at least ten minutes before I finally got up on the podium to receive the cup. Gary Teichmann had done an interview over the Tannoy in the meantime, but the South Africans couldn't wait to get off the pitch. After all, it must have really stuck in their throats to see us getting presented with the trophy at Ellis Park of all places! When the presentation was finally over I was supposed to give an interview, but I just ducked off the podium and started the lap of honour; I wasn't interested in talking at that moment. I was much happier walking around the stadium waving a Union Jack that someone had thrown at me. It was a brilliant moment. There were thousands of red and white shirts in the place and no one could possibly have imagined this scene two years previously. Back then everyone had been watching the World Cup final, Nelson Mandela was wearing François Pienaar's number six shirt and South Africa had been crowned champions. Now we'd taken over, all the locals had gone home and we had the place to ourselves. Brilliant. Actually, at least one South African must have stayed because I was hit on the leg by an orange that had been thrown at me in disgust or frustration. It was very tasty, as it happens!

I knew from gestures like that just how hacked off the South

Africans were that we'd won the series. They genuinely thought that Northern Hemisphere rugby was way behind their own, even though they never really watched it. They expected us to play some boring, ten-man rugby game and really believed we wouldn't mount a serious challenge. I think they found it very hard to take when they weren't the ones larging it as the winners. Not that I was going to lose too many hours' sleep worrying about them.

When I finally left the field I headed for the dressing-room. It was relatively quiet, in fact, with some people taking in what we'd achieved and savouring it, whilst others were probably a bit cheesed off because we'd lost the match. Overall it was probably a bit subdued again because everyone was experiencing that strange cocktail of being very happy yet totally exhausted. I had to attend to a cut on the face that needed a couple of stitches. It was not a pretty sight down in the treatment room, I can tell you. Jerry was moping about with his arm, Jason Leonard was in there getting something or other seen to, and there were three or four Scots fans in kilts who'd twisted their ankles. My surgeon Dr Gilmore had flown down from London for the game and had decided that it was time to check on the old groin problem again. The way he checks on it is to feel for a certain point right underneath the scrotum, which is absolute agony if the problem hasn't cleared up. Needless to say it hadn't, and I had to suffer both pain and ignominy in front of an appreciative audience of people killing themselves laughing. I couldn't help thinking that something wasn't quite right. I hadn't written this into my imaginary script of what it would be like captaining a victorious Lions side! I told Gilmore that I'd see him back in London on Thursday for the operation and gingerly headed back upstairs for the press conference.

There wasn't much to be said to the world's press, really. I talked about the game, said that we'd perhaps played better rugby than we had previously but hadn't taken our chances, and gave the South Africans credit for playing well. There was no doubt about it; they'd been the better team. I didn't make any public comment about it, but I was glad that the tour had finally come to an end. It's probably a psychological thing, but I was mentally drained and felt that I'd had enough. I knew that this was where the tour ended so I was probably prepared for it and was ready to relax. If someone had come up to me then and said that I'd have to do another four weeks, I don't know if

I would have been able to cope. If I'd known all along that there would be another four weeks, though, I would probably have sailed through it. The mind operates in strange ways.

I then went to make the obligatory speeches for the dignitaries and tried to have a chat with some of the Springboks who were milling around. They seemed a bit stand-offish, to be blunt. I had a few words with Gary Teichmann, but I wouldn't like to judge him on the strength of that brief conversation. The rest of our boys had wanted to get going, but I thought that it would be courteous and polite to stay around for a while. I was disappointed that most of the people we'd been playing against these last three Tests didn't really want to know, but I wouldn't say I was particularly bothered by it. I know that they are decent enough guys, probably not much different from our lads having had the same backgrounds playing rugby and loving the sport. I've spoken to blokes like Mark Andrews and André Joubert in the past and got on okay with them, and even players who didn't make the Test side like Kobus Wiese, who looks like a real animal on the pitch, is a very nice guy indeed. It was just the circumstances and probably the pressure that the Springboks were under to succeed that meant we didn't have much of a relationship with them. So be it.

Once we'd arrived back at the hotel at about ten o'clock, everyone gathered in the team room for the last official meeting before we all signed off the tour. Fran got up and delivered a speech of sorts, although to be truthful I can't remember much of what he said. He did talk about what we'd achieved and what a good bunch of guys we were, which probably didn't really need saying but was a good thing to do anyway. I got to my feet and thanked the management for all their input over the tour, and I meant it. I thought they'd done a magnificent job and there was no way we would have been as successful if Fran, Geech and Jim hadn't been so good in every department. I'm not sure that the rest of the guys were too interested in me waffling on by this time, though. They were far more keen to get away and do whatever it was they wanted to do. Again, people weren't swinging from the chandeliers with the excitement of it all; that was just the way we reacted to what had happened and I can't really explain it.

The extent of my own celebrations on the night were a quiet meal in the hotel with Kay, then sitting around having a few drinks with some friends of ours. My mum and dad were still both down in South Africa, but I didn't get together with them on that night. It wasn't the craziest evening I've ever had in my life, but I went to bed feeling both happy and satisfied all the same. Job done, as they say.

CHAPTER NINETEEN

Home

I woke up late-ish on the Sunday and savoured the prospect of not having any training or official functions to think about. Kay and I wandered down to the shops and mooched about a bit, just killing time, really. She was flying back to Britain later on that day and I wanted to spend some time with her, so we just popped into the lunchtime affair that Scottish Provident had organised for the squad for a short while. I had an idea that a few beers might be getting sunk, so I thought I'd best not hang around too long.

After dropping Kay off at the airport and telling her that I'd see her back in Britain, I still had one commitment left to attend to. I'd agreed to do a photo session in the early evening for a South African motoring magazine. It was a bit strange really. They were doing a head-to-head testing thing with a Ford Fiesta and a Vauxhall Corsa, and I was kind of facing off against the Springbok lock Hannes Strydom. He seemed like a decent enough bloke, but in all honesty it was too cold out at the shoot to get heavily into any social niceties and I was just glad to get back again around eight o'clock.

I decided I might as well go to the Scot Prov do and see if there were any signs of life. It seemed like most of the boys had been trying to drink the entire profits of one particular life assurance company and had made a pretty good show of it. Most of them were in bits or in bed. Hilly was wandering around gibbering on about how he'd lost his mobile phone and Taity was going on about what a bad state he was in. I must admit that I didn't think he looked all that bad, but I suppose he knew best. My plans for the evening went a bit west, though. I was up for a night out, but there weren't that many takers and I ended up having a couple of quiet ones not too far from the hotel, and turning in reasonably early.

I couldn't really believe that my final day in South Africa had come around. I'd been so used to the routine of the tour that the idea of going home, back to normality, hadn't really sunk in. I took my mind off things by going out to the South African mint in Pretoria to pick up all the quarter krugerrands that we'd bought as mementoes with the money from the players' kitty. Fran and Allan Bateman came with me and we were given a guided tour of the place. They showed us these huge machines that knock out the coins from sheets of precious metals, but I reckon that once you've seen one mint, you've seen 'em all, and I wasn't that bothered when we left for the hotel and one last packing of the bags.

Saying goodbye to the English lads – Jason Leonard, Tony Diprose, Graham Rowntree and the others – at Johannesburg airport was quite difficult. I'm a professional rugby player and when I see the rest of my team-mates heading off somewhere else to represent their country, my natural reaction is to want to be going on with them. Jerry Guscott was on the plane back to England with me, though, not only because of the injury he'd picked up on Saturday, but also because his wife had given birth to a baby daughter while we were away and he'd decided that he should be back home with her. I knew that I was making the right decision to get my groin sorted, really, and so was resigned to preparing myself for the long flight back to London.

Virgin had changed the enormous V from the logo that was painted on the tail of the jumbo into a victory salute, which was a nice touch. I wasn't really aware of how much our performances down in South Africa had affected people back home, so it was good to see that people were so excited about what we'd achieved. Virgin couldn't do enough for us again, which meant that we had a comfortable time on the way back home. They actually made a cake for Jerry because it was his birthday, and I think a few of the lads had a bit of a party on the plane with him. Me? I'll give you one guess what I was doing as soon as I sat down in my seat. I was in the land of nod until just before we touched down at Heathrow.

I knew that there was a press conference arranged for us at the airport and that it would be my last official duty as Lions captain. By this time I'd totally lost it. I was tired and wanted to get myself home as quickly as possible, but I had to put a brave face on things and talk to the press about the tour in general. It was a bit of a weird affair, because most of the country's rugby journalists were on a plane to Australia, so the room that was hired for the conference was half-empty. There were, however, plenty of TV cameras around and Jerry, Fran, Geech and I did the honours as best we could. The questions we were asked were pretty mindless – 'Are you pleased to have won the series?' 'Was it difficult down in South Africa?' – so I was glad when I was finally done and could get myself out of there. One of the directors from my management company had also come back from South Africa on the same flight and he gave me a lift back to Oatlands in Weybridge where I'd left my car for the past seven weeks.

Once I'd got hold of my Scorpio I had to head back into London to pick Kay up. She'd had a disastrous flight back home, coming down with food poisoning during her stopover in Zurich, but some friends she'd made during her time in South Africa took her back to their place in the Isle of Dogs and looked after her. I had a good time on the way down to get her, actually. I cut right across the centre of town, crossing the Thames by the Houses of Parliament with the radio blaring. I was listening to some good music, it was a beautiful Tuesday afternoon and I hadn't driven in ages, so I didn't even mind being stuck in a traffic jam. It's funny, the way you don't realise how much you've missed being in your own country until you finally get back home.

Kay was feeling a lot better by the time I picked her up and the drive back up to our new home near Leicester was very pleasant. There was only one thing that I'd set my heart on doing as soon as I got back – eating fish and chips. I hadn't eaten any since I'd been away and I was more than happy to drive the extra four miles out of my way to get hold of some. I think I would have crawled over broken glass for it, I was so desperate. Once I got through the front door of the house I grabbed some salad cream from the kitchen, poured a whole load over my food and sat down to eat. Just one solitary thought entered my head as I chewed away. It had been great to go away, and it had been a wonderful experience leading the Lions to victory, one that will stay with me forever. But there was no doubt about it: it was great to be back home. As a winning captain.

CHAPTER TWENTY

The Lions Legacy

With the benefit of hindsight I can still look back on the British Lions' tour to South Africa with a great deal of pride. The general consensus before we left the UK was that our rugby was a long, long way behind South Africa's, that the Southern Hemisphere sides were more than capable of overrunning teams from the Northern Hemisphere and that it was a foregone conclusion that we'd lose the series. We don't have the Super 12 tournament and it's probably true that the top five club sides in the world are from the South, but despite the perceived gap we proved to everybody that we can play with the best and compete with them. The thing is, though, that there's no huge secret to the way those countries play the game of rugby; they just have a massive physical commitment to the game. If you can match them head to head in that department then you're always going to stand a chance, because players up here aren't naturally less gifted ball-players. And if you think back to the games, there were times in the Test matches when we definitely had the edge on the Springboks in terms of pure physicality. Most people would agree that Scott Gibbs was the hardest tackler in the entire series, but I think the Lions competed in every area of the pitch. The back row was fantastic. The Springboks thought that they'd dominate at the scrum and after we got our act together early in the tour they never did. We proved what could be achieved and that the way to achieve it was simply to do what we already were doing, but do it better.

Looking at the broader picture, it's easy to see that the tour has done a lot of good in raising rugby union's profile in this country. Any successful sports team will get media attention. People might say that the fact that none of the games or even highlights were shown on terrestrial TV because the rights had been assigned exclusively to *Sky* will have held us back, but that's not the entire issue. There's no doubt that you have to make a positive choice to pay for Sky Sports, and the casual viewers who maybe only ever watch rugby when the Five Nations is on *Grandstand* once a year have missed out on seeing some great games. But there's no way that the BBC or ITV, whoever, would have shown every game of the tour live the way Sky did, nor would they have pumped as much money into the game as Sky. Rugby can build on the groundwork of the Lions tour, because there's more money available to improve the sport and I think it's an inevitable consequence of the way that sport in general is developing that there will soon be a far greater choice of sporting events to watch. But let's not kid ourselves. It will necessarily mean that we'll all have to pay for the privilege of watching it. Sky has the money and sporting bodies will accept their bids. Sport is becoming more élitist and people are only interested in games and events of the very highest quality, but that means that standards will be raised.

If British rugby is going to survive then it needs a strong domestic competition, it needs to increase its profile and it needs to market itself better. After all, there's no doubt that this is a game that attracts a core audience of people who are already attractive to advertisers – the young, educated and reasonably well-off. The sport just needs more of them. The BBC's coverage to date has concentrated on presenting rugby as a low-key affair. That's not the way to get new people interested. Rugby's a high-impact sport that thrives on intense physical confrontation. When we made that point before we left for South Africa and said that we would compete with the Springboks at that level, the press tried to turn what we'd said into something cynical, as if we were only interested in fighting. That's not what we were trying to say at all, but the intense confrontation and the fast action is what's exciting about the game.

The last domestic league season was by far the best I've ever played in in terms of quality, and if it keeps on improving at the rate it has done then people will soon realise that rugby's a brilliant sport to watch. That will take a bit of time, but we need general sports fans to believe that club rugby matters, and that's not the case at the moment. Most people who might have taken a casual interest in the Lions tour would be hard-pressed to name the club sides that any of us play for. That's down to the history of British rugby. *Rugby Special* on BBC2 was the only means of contact that most people had with club rugby, and no wonder they couldn't get excited about it. The presentation was boring, the standard of play was low and there was nobody in the crowd to create an atmosphere. I rarely watched it myself and I'm a player! It was usually a question of watching a low-fitness, low-skill-level game in a park. Sports fans want glamour and the Lions tour had it. We were playing games in world-class stadiums and the whole thing looked sexy. I remember sitting in the hotel in Durban watching the lads play up in the Free State, and everyone had the same feeling – that it looked superb and we all wished we were playing. It gave everyone a buzz. Even the Five Nations, supposedly our premier rugby tournament, has been lacking in skill and 'watchability' – and I'm guilty of contributing to that.

Whenever I used to play for England I always said I didn't care about doing things for the crowds. I played to enjoy the game myself and I wasn't too bothered about the spectators. My attitude had changed a lot since we've become professionals, because I know that the watchability of the game on television will have a direct impact on my being paid to play rugby. If we, the players, don't make the game exciting, then at the end of the day we'll be the ones who'll suffer. And I make no bones about admitting that I like being in a sport that's getting a higher profile all the time.

I believe that I was lucky to get into rugby at all given the way the sport was presented when I was growing up. If my parents hadn't moved from Birmingham to Leicester when I was young it's entirely possible that I might not have taken an interest in the game. Most rugby matches just seemed to be nothing more than a load of fat blokes running about in kit that looked old and tatty and with socks that didn't even match! Leicester was the one exception to the rule, a club that really had its act together and had a team that was packed with England players performing in front of big crowds. From the age of 12 or 13 I wanted to play for Leicester because I loved the glamour of the club, yet I think there are hardly any other rugby players who could honestly say that they dreamed of playing for a club side when they were younger.

Even at international level I can see positive benefits from the Lions tour, especially for England. The sheer volume of players who were out there and who gained invaluable experience is incredible. Tony Underwood played some of the best rugby of his life, Tim Stimpson came through as someone who can be world class, Matt Dawson showed exactly what he can do at the very highest level and there were plenty of other players who will have improved because of their experiences out in South Africa.

I'm glad to see that everything to do with rugby is now stepping up a gear. Wasps are playing their home games down at the QPR football ground and Saracens have moved to Watford. The quality of these stadiums makes it look like the sides who play in them mean business and even the kits the sides are wearing are cool. The sport is growing quickly, it's an exciting time for rugby and I think that this can only be good for the sport in general and for the standard of the game we play here.

The whole South African experience will act as a great springboard for the second season of professionalism. Almost every club has some-one or other who was out on the tour who will be telling all the players how much more fulfilling it is and how much more enjoyment you get out of the game when you're playing against top-class athletes at the very highest of levels. Every game that I played in South Africa gave me a buzz and that hasn't always been the way of things in our domestic league. There was a time when you'd only get that real high on two or three occasions a season. I wouldn't mind betting that by the end of next season, with even more tough European games in the schedule, there's no way I'll be saying the same thing.

The only dark clouds on the horizon are the constant problems that keep cropping up with the RFU and their relationships with indivi-duals and clubs. The game is moving at a rate of knots now that professionalism is starting to pick up, and it needs everyone to get on board for the benefit and the advancement of the game. Otherwise fights and squabbles will tear the game apart. And nobody wants that to happen.

On a personal level I really can't complain. The money I earn from the game is great and I'm very happy to be well paid for what I do. Getting a big cheque for doing something you love has no downside, but I feel comfortable about the situation because I was doing exactly the same things and had reached the same level before I was a professional. I've never been motivated to play rugby to earn money, and I'm still not. I just love playing and striving to be the best. That's why I wasn't unduly concerned by people writing the Lions off before the tour. I thought we could do it and it made me very proud to prove a lot of doubters wrong. In many ways those people made me even stronger as a leader and as a player. After we won the first Test I was more determined than ever not to let the South Africans back into the series. In many ways that would have been even worse than not winning any of the Tests, because people would have been really patronising. They would have said things like 'There, there. You nearly did it.' I would have hated that.

If I were asked whether or not I was a good captain of the British Lions, I'm still not sure how I'd answer. I'd certainly hope that the people who played under me would at least say that I wasn't a bad captain. I suppose I'd say that I was adequate, but the truth of the matter is that with the attitude that players have to have these days, their dedication to the game, their fitness and their all-round professionalism, the captain's role is probably not as important or as influential as it once was. I've thought about this a bit and I'm still convinced it's true. I believe that the British Lions squad in South Africa could most likely have survived the loss of any one player and still achieved the same series victory. And I include myself in that assessment. The proof of the pudding lies in the fact that we lost Rob Howley, who was probably the only player who was generally acknowledged as being pretty much guaranteed his Test position. When we lost Rob through injury just before the first Test I was worried about whether we could come back from such a bitter blow, but Matt Dawson scored the try that set up our victory in Cape Town and performed superbly throughout the rest of the tour.

Other players whom many people probably wouldn't have even heard of before the tour also came through. Paul Wallace, whose scrummaging I mentioned earlier, proved himself a key man, and Jerry Davidson performed heroically in the line-out. When we lost Tony Underwood and Jerry Guscott in the third Test, Tim Stimpson and Allan Bateman performed brilliantly in the second half. There was such great strength in depth that it stands to reason that we could have sustained any loss and come through unscathed. The whole tour really was a team effort and as captain I suppose I was just the figurehead.

There wasn't a stage in the tour that I could pinpoint where things had reached crisis point. There weren't any deep, dark nights when I was forced to do a lot of soul-searching. The match against Gauteng was a vital fixture for us, coming off the back of our defeat against Northern Transvaal, but even then I still believed that we could have lost that match and then gone on to win the series. There was never really a moment where the captain's role was to step in, pull people up by their bootlaces and get them through. Things went so well on the tour that the momentum built up and carried us all through — and much of the credit must go to the management team for that.

I wouldn't say that I know Fran Cotton particularly well after the tour. We only really spoke about rugby, but whenever we did speak I always found him to be very down-to-earth and sensible. I wasn't bothered that he didn't want to be my mate; I'm quite reserved when it comes to embarking upon friendships too. What I do know about Fran is that everything he did on tour was designed to benefit the players and to help them win the Test matches. He wasn't a man who liked speaking just to hear the sound of his own voice. He's a man who desperately wants our rugby to be successful and he's very determined about doing what he can to ensure that happens. I'm sure that won't change now that the Lions tour is over, and his influence in the game will continue to be massive. He certainly wasn't down in South Africa for the benefit of his own ego and I respected his organisational skills immensely. Geech was in a class of his own, too. Anyone who has coached the Lions to two winning series has proved himself to be a legend, and he's now a massive part of the British Lions' folklore and history. I thought Geech was a great bloke and worked superbly with both Fran and Jim Telfer. Out on the training field Geech and Jim were ideal coaching partners. They're completely different people – Jim's far more fiery than Geech – but they complement each other superbly. The overall management blend was brilliant, and thanks to them all that the rest of the lads and I had to do was concentrate on playing. And winning. And that's exactly what we did.

APPENDIX ONE

The British Lions' Itinerary, South Africa 1997

Sunday 18 May
10.00 Arrive at Johannesburg International Airport on Virgin
       Atlantic flight VS601
       After an official welcome, followed by a media conference, the
       touring party will depart for Durban
14.00 Depart Johannesburg International Airport for Durban on
       flight SA 533
15.00 Arrive at Durban International Airport and transfer to the
       Beverley Hills Intercontinental for a five-night stay

Monday 19 May
Day of training and leisure

Tuesday 20 May
Day of training and leisure

Wednesday 21 May
Media open day
All members of the media are invited to join the Lions for a welcome
    braai at the hotel
Day of training and leisure

Thursday 22 May
Day of training and leisure

Friday 23 May
Durban/Port Elizabeth
16.00 Depart hotel
17.30 Depart Durban International Airport for Port Elizabeth on

flight SA 623
18.50 Arrive at Port Elizabeth Airport and transfer to the Holiday
Inn Garden Court, King's Beach, for a two-night stay

Saturday 24 May
10.00 Coaching clinic at Adcock Stadium, Port Elizabeth
13.00 Depart hotel for Telkom Park
15.15 Lions vs. Eastern Province Invitation XV
17.30 After-match function
19.00 ETD from Telkom Park to the hotel
19.45 ETA at the hotel

Sunday 25 May
Port Elizabeth/East London
14.00 Depart hotel for Port Elizabeth Airport
15.05 Depart Port Elizabeth Airport for East London on flight SA
427
16.00 Arrive at East London Airport and transfer to the Holiday Inn
Garden Court, East London, for a four-night stay
17.00 ETA at the hotel

Monday 26 May
Day of training and leisure

Tuesday May 27
Day of training and leisure

Wednesday 28 May
13.20 Depart hotel for Basil Kenyon Stadium
15.15 Lions vs. Border
17.30 After-match function
19.00 ETD from Basil Kenyon Stadium to the hotel
19.45 ETA at the hotel

Thursday 29 May
East London/Cape Town
13.00 Depart hotel for East London Airport for Cape Town on
flight SA 1351

16.00 Arrive at Cape Town International Airport and transfer to the
Holiday Inn Garden Court, Newlands, for a three-night stay
17.00 ETA at the hotel

Friday 30 May
Day of training and leisure

Saturday 31 May
13.30 Depart hotel for Norwich Park Stadium, Newlands
15.15 Lions vs. Western Province
17.30 After-match function
19.00 ETD from Norwich Park, Newlands, to the hotel

Sunday 1 June
Cape Town/Johannesburg
13.00 Depart hotel for Cape Town International Airport
14.35 Depart Cape Town International Airport for Johannesburg on
flight SA 324
16.30 Arrive at Johannesburg International Airport and transfer to
the Holiday Inn Crowne Plaza, Pretoria, for an 11-night stay
17.30 ETA at the hotel

Monday 2 June
Day of training and leisure

Tuesday 3 June
Day of training and leisure

Wednesday 4 June
Pretoria/Witbank/Pretoria
By road to Witbank and return to Pretoria
10.30 Depart hotel by road transport to Witbank
12.00 ETA at the Boulevard Hotel, Witbank
12.15 Lunch at the Boulevard Hotel
13.30 Depart hotel for Johann van Riebeeck Stadium
15.15 Lions vs. Mpumalanga (formerly S.E. Transvaal)
17.30 After-match function
19.00 ETD from Witbank to Pretoria

20.00 ETA at the hotel

Thursday 5 June
Day of training and leisure

Friday 6 June
Day of training and leisure

Saturday 7 June
13.00 Depart hotel for the Loftus Versfeld Stadium
15.15 vs. Northern Transvaal
17.30 After-match function
19.00 ETD from Loftus Versfeld Stadium to the hotel
19.15 ETA at the hotel

Sunday 8 June
Day of training and leisure

Monday 9 June
Day of training and leisure

Tuesday 10 June
Day of training and leisure

Wednesday 11 June
Pretoria/Johannesburg/Pretoria
16.45 Depart hotel for Ellis Park Stadium
19.15 Lions vs. Gauteng Lions (formerly Transvaal)
21.30 After-match function
22.30 ETD from Ellis Park Stadium to the hotel
23.30 ETA at the hotel

Thursday 12 June
Johannesburg/Durban
15.30 Depart Johannesburg International Airport for Durban on
       flight SA 539
16.30 Arrive at Durban International Airport and transfer to the
       Beverley Hills Intercontinental Hotel for a three-night stay

17.15 ETA at the hotel

Friday 13 June
Day of training and leisure

Saturday 14 June
13.30 Depart hotel for The Stadium, King's Park
15.15 Lions vs. Natal
17.30 After-match function
19.00 ETD from The Stadium, King's Park to the hotel
19.15 ETA at the hotel

Sunday 15 June
Durban/Cape Town
13.00 Depart hotel for Durban International Airport
14.25 Depart Durban International Airport for Cape Town on flight
       SA 635
16.40 Arrive at Cape Town International Airport and transfer to the
       Holiday Inn Garden Court, Newlands, for a seven-night stay
17.30 ETA at the hotel

Monday 16 June
Day of training and leisure

Tuesday 17 June
Cape Town/Wellington/Cape Town
By road to Wellington and return to Cape Town
11.45 Brunch
12.45 Depart hotel by road transport
13.45 ETA in Wellington
15.15 Lions vs. Emerging Springboks
17.30 After-match function
18.30 ETD from Wellington to Cape Town
19.30 ETA at the hotel

Wednesday 18 June
Day of training and leisure

Thursday 19 June
Day of training and leisure

Friday 20 June
Day of training and leisure

Saturday 21 June
15.30 Depart hotel
17.15 Lions vs. South Africa (First Test)
19.30 After-match function
21.00 ETD from Norwich Park, Newlands, to the hotel

Sunday 22 June
Cape Town/Durban
13.15 Depart hotel for Cape Town International Airport
14.30 Depart Cape Town International Airport for Durban on flight
         SA 630
16.25 Arrive at Durban International Airport and transfer to the
         Holiday Inn Crowne Plaza, Durban, for an eight-night stay
18.00 ETA at the hotel

Monday 23 June
Day of training and leisure

Tuesday 24 June
Durban/Bloemfontein
11.30 Depart hotel for Durban International Airport
13.15 Charter flight for 30 people departs Durban International
         Airport for Bloemfontein
14.30 Arrive at Bloemfontein Airport and transfer to the Holiday
         Inn Garden Court, Bloemfontein, for a one-night stay
15.00 ETA at the hotel
17.45 Depart hotel for Free State Stadium
19.15 Lions vs. Free State
21.30 After-match function
23.30 ETD from Free State Stadium to hotel
23.40 ETA at hotel

Wednesday 25 June
Bloemfontein/Durban
07.00 Depart hotel for Bloemfontein Airport
08.30 Charter flight for 30 people departs Bloemfontein Airport for Durban
10.45 Arrive at Durban International Airport and transfer to the Holiday Inn Crowne Plaza, Durban, to join up with the rest of the team

Thursday 26 June
Day of training and leisure

Friday 27 June
Day of training and leisure

Saturday 28 June
15.15 Depart hotel for The Stadium, King's Park
17.15 The Lions vs. South Africa (Second Test)
19.30 After-match function
21.00 ETD from The Stadium, King's Park to the hotel
21.15 ETA at the hotel

Sunday 29 June
Durban/Johannesburg
12.30 Depart hotel for Durban International Airport
14.00 Depart Durban International Airport for Johannesburg on flight SA 520
15.00 Arrive at Johannesburg International Airport and transfer to the Riverside Sun for a four night-stay
16.30 ETA at the hotel

Monday 30 June
Day of training and leisure

Tuesday 1 July
Riverside/Welkom/Riverside
By road to Welkom and return to Riverside
09.30 Depart hotel by road transport to Welkom Inn (30 people)

11.30 ETA at the Welkom Inn
12.00 Lunch at the Welkom Inn
13.30 Depart hotel for North West Stadium
15.15 Lions vs. Northern Free State
17.30 After-match function
19.00 ETD from Welkom to Riverside
21.00 ETA at the hotel

Wednesday 2 July
Riverside/Johannesburg
a.m. Training
p.m. Transfer to Holiday Inn Crowne Plaza, Sandton, by road (coach)

Thursday 3 July
Day of training and leisure

Friday 4 July
Day of training and leisure

Saturday 5 July
15.00 Depart hotel for Ellis Park Stadium
17.15 Lions vs. South Africa (Third Test)
19.30 After-match function
21.00 ETD from Ellis Park Stadium to the hotel
21.30 ETA at the hotel

Sunday 6 July
Day of leisure

Monday 7 July
18.00 Depart hotel for Johannesburg International Airport
20.15 Depart Johannesburg International Airport on Virgin Atlantic
       flight VS 602 for London

APPENDIX TWO

The British Lions in South Africa 1997: Teams and Results

Saturday 24 May
Versus Eastern Province Invitation XV at Telkom Park, Port Elizabeth
Won 39–11
TEAMS
Eastern Province Invitation XV
T. van Rensburg, D. Keyser, R. van Jaarsveld, H. le Roux, H. Pedro,
K. Ford (R. Fourie, 42), C. Alcock, D. Saayman, G. Kirsten (Capt)
(M. Winter, 80), W. Enslin (W. Lessing, 38), M. Webber (M. van der
Merwe, 44), J. Wiese, A. du Preez, S. Scott-Young, J. Greeff
British Lions
N. Jenkins, I. Evans (T. Underwood, 67), J. Guscott, W. Greenwood,
N. Beal, G. Townsend, R. Howley, T. Smith, K. Wood (B. Williams,
67), J. Leonard (Capt), L. Dallaglio, G. Weir, S. Shaw (J. Davidson,
77), R. Hill, S. Quinnell
SCORERS
Eastern Province Invitational XV
Try: Keyser
Penalty goals: van Rensburg (2)
British Lions
Tries: Guscott (2), Weir, Underwood, Greenwood
Conversions: Jenkins (4)
Penalty goals: Jenkins (2)

Wednesday 28 May
Versus Border at Basil Kenyon Stadium, East London
Won 18–14

TEAMS
Border
R. Bennett, K. Hilton-Green, G. Hechter, K. Malotana (D. Maidza, 42), A. Claassen, G. Miller, J. Bradbrook, H. Kok, R. van Zyl (Capt), D. du Preez, M. Swart, S. Botha, J. Gehring, A. Botha (D. Coetzer, 79), A. Fox
British Lions
T. Stimpson, J. Bentley, A. Bateman, S. Gibbs (A. Tait, 46), T. Underwood, P. Grayson, A. Healey (M. Dawson, 55), G. Rowntree, M. Regan, D. Young (P. Wallace, 68), R. Wainwright (Capt), G Weir, J. Davidson, N. Back, E. Miller
SCORERS
Border
Try: Claasen
Penalty goals: Miller (3)
British Lions
Tries: Bentley, Regan, Wainwright
Penalty goal: Stimpson

Saturday 31 May
Versus Western Province at Norwich Park, Newlands, Cape Town
Won 38–21
TEAMS
Western Province
J. Swart, J. Small, R. Fleck, R. Muir (Capt), S. Berridge, P. Montgomery, S. Hatley, G. Pagel (A. van der Linde ,61), A. Paterson, K. Andrews, R. Brink, F. van Heerden, H. Louw, C. Krige (R. Skinstad, 66), A. Aitken
British Lions
T. Stimpson, I. Evans, J. Guscott, A. Tait (W. Greenwood, 74), J. Bentley, G. Townsend, R. Howley, G. Rowntree, B. Williams, J. Leonard, L. Dallaglio, M. Johnson (Capt), S. Shaw, R. Hill, T. Rodber (S. Quinnell, 63)
SCORERS
Western Province
Tries: Muir (2), Brink
Conversions: Montgomery (3)

British Lions
Tries: Bentley (2), Tait, Evans
Conversions: Stimpson (3)
Penalty goals: Stimpson (4)

Wednesday 4 June
Versus Mpumalanga at Johann van Riebeeck Stadium, Witbank
Won 64–14
TEAMS
Mpumalanga
E. Gericke, J. Visagie, R. Potgieter, G. Gendall, P. Nel (A. van
Rooyen, 76), R. van As, D. van Zyl, H. Swart, H. Kemp, A. Botha,
F. Rossouw, E. van der Berg, M. Bosman, P. Joubert, T. Oosthuizen
(Capt) (J. Buekes, 71)
British Lions
N. Beal, I. Evans, A. Bateman, W. Greenwood, T. Underwood,
N. Jenkins, M. Dawson, T. Smith, K. Wood (M. Regan, 52),
P. Wallace (D. Young, 74), R. Wainwright, G. Weir (S. Shaw, 67),
J. Davidson, N. Back, T. Rodber (Capt)
SCORERS
Mpumalanga
Tries: Joubert (2)
Conversions: van As (2)
British Lions
Tries: Wainwright (3), Evans (2), Underwood (2), Dawson, Jenkins,
Beal
Conversions: Jenkins (7)

Saturday 7 June
Versus Northern Transvaal at Loftus Versfeld Stadium, Pretoria
Lost 30–35
TEAMS
Northern Transvaal
G. Bouwer, W. Lourens (G. Esterhuizen, 34), J. Schutte, D. van
Schalkwyk, C. Steyn, R. de Marigny, C. Breytenbach, L. Campher,
H. Tromp (J. Brooks, 40), P. Boer (J. Taljaard, 71), D. Grobbelaar
(G. Laufs, 39), D. Badenhorst (R. Schroeder 63), N. van der Walt,
A. Richter (Capt), S. Bekker

British Lions
T. Stimpson, J. Bentley (S. Gibbs, 58), J. Guscott, A. Tait,
T. Underwood, G. Townsend, R. Howley, G. Rowntree, M. Regan,
J. Leonard (D. Young, 75), M. Johnson (Capt), S. Shaw, L. Dallaglio,
S. Quinnell, E. Miller
SCORERS
Northern Transvaal
Tries: Steyn, van Schalkwyk (2), Richter
Conversions: Steyn (3)
Penalty goals: Steyn (3)
British Lions
Tries: Guscott (2), Townsend
Conversions: Stimpson (3)
Penalty goals: Stimpson (3)

Wednesday 11 June
Versus Gauteng Lions at Ellis Park Stadium, Johannesburg
Won: 20–14
TEAMS
Gauteng Lions
D. du Toit, J. Gillingham, J. van der Walt, H. le Roux, P. Hendriks,
L. van Rensburg, J. Roux, R. Grau (B. Swart, 60), C. Rossouw
(J. Dalton, 52), K. van Greuning, A. Vos, J. Wiese (Capt),
B. Thorne, P. Krause, W. Brosnihan
British Lions
N. Beal, J. Bentley, J. Guscott, W. Greenwood, T. Underwood
(N. Jenkins, 57), M. Catt, A. Healey, T. Smith, B. Williams,
P. Wallace, R. Wainwright, N. Redman, J. Davidson, N. Back,
T. Rodber (Capt)
SCORERS
Gauteng Lions
Try: Vos
Penalty goals: du Toit (3)
British Lions
Tries: Healey, Bentley
Conversions: Jenkins (2)
Penalty goals: Catt, Jenkins

Saturday 14 June
Versus Natal at The Stadium, King's Park, Durban
Won 42–12
TEAMS
Natal
G. Lawless, S. Payne, J. Thomson, P. Muller, J. Joubert, H. Scriba,
R. du Preez, O. le Roux (J. Smit, 67), J. Allan, R. Kempson,
N. Wegner, J. Slade, W. van Heerden (R. Strudwick, 29), W. Fyvie
(Capt), D. Kriese
British Lions
N. Jenkins, I. Evans, A. Bateman (M. Catt, 66), S. Gibbs, A. Tait,
G. Townsend, R. Howley (M. Dawson, 12), T. Smith (J. Leonard,
68), K. Wood, D. Young, M. Johnson (Capt), S. Shaw, L. Dallaglio,
R. Hill, E. Miller
SCORERS
Natal
Penalty goals: Lawless (4)
British Lions
Tries: Townsend, Dallaglio, Catt
Conversions: Jenkins (3)
Penalty goals: Jenkins (6)
Drop goals: Townsend

Tuesday 17 June
Versus Emerging Springboks at Boland Stadium, Wellington
Won 51–22
TEAMS
Emerging Springboks
M. Smith, D. Kayser, P. Montgomery, M. Hendricks, P. Treu, L. van
Rensburg (M. Goosen, 23), J. Adlam (K. Myburgh, 11), R. Kempson
(L. Campher, 68), D. Santon (Capt), N. du Toit, W. Brosnihan
(T. Arendse, 71), R. Opperman, B. Els, P. Smit (K. Malotana, 67),
J. Coetzee.
British Lions
T. Stimpson, J. Bentley, A. Bateman, W. Greenwood, N. Beal,
M. Catt, A. Healey, G. Rowntree, M. Regan, J. Leonard (Capt),
R. Wainwright, N. Redman, J. Davidson, N. Back, A. Diprose

SCORERS
Emerging Springboks
Tries: Brosnihan, Goosen, Treu
Conversions: Smith, Montgomery
Penalty goal: Smith
British Lions
Tries: Beal (3), Rowntree, Stimpson, Catt
Conversions: Stimpson (6)
Penalty goals: Stimpson (3)

Saturday 21 June
Versus South Africa at Norwich Park, Newlands, Cape Town
Won 25–16
TEAMS
South Africa
A. Joubert, J. Small, J. Mulder, E Lubbe (R. Bennett, 40),
A. Snyman, H. Honiball, J. van der Westhuizen, O. du Randt,
N. Drotske, A. Garvey, M. Andrews, H. Strydom, R. Kruger,
G. Teichmann (Capt), A. Venter
British Lions
N. Jenkins, I. Evans, S. Gibbs, J. Guscott, A. Tait, G. Townsend,
M. Dawson, T. Smith (J. Leonard, 79), K. Wood, P. Wallace,
M. Johnson (Capt), J. Davidson, L. Dallaglio, T. Rodber, R. Hill
SCORERS
South Africa
Tries: du Randt, Bennett
Penalty goals: Lubbe, Honiball
British Lions
Tries: Dawson, Tait
Penalty goals: Jenkins (5)

Tuesday 24 June
Versus Free State at Free State Stadium, Bloemfontein
Won 52–30
TEAMS
Free State
M. Smith, J-H van Wyk, H. Muller (Capt), B. Venter, S. Brink, J. de
Beer, S. Fourie (H. Jacobs, 40), D. Groenewald, C. Marais, W. Meyer

(D. Heymans, 60), C. van Rensburg, R. Opperman, B. Els,
J. Erasmus, J. Coetzee
British Lions
T. Stimpson, J. Bentley, A. Bateman, W. Greenwood (N. Jenkins,
40), T. Underwood, M. Catt, A. Healey, G. Rowntree (J. Leonard,
73), B. Williams, D. Young, R. Wainwright, N. Redman (Capt),
S. Shaw, N. Back, E. Miller
SCORERS
Free State
Tries: Brink (2), de Beer
Conversions: de Beer (3)
Penalty goals: de Beer (3)
British Lions
Tries: Bentley (3), Stimpson, Bateman, Jenkins, Underwood
Conversions: Stimpson (4)
Penalty goal: Stimpson (3)

Saturday 28 June
Versus South Africa at The Stadium, King's Park, Durban
Won 18–15
TEAMS
South Africa
A. Joubert, A. Snyman, P. Montgomery, D. van Schalkwyk,
P. Rossouw, H. Honiball, J. van der Westhuizen, O. du Randt,
N. Drotske, A. Garvey (D. Theron, 67), H. Strydom, M. Andrews,
R. Kruger (F. van Heerden, 50), G. Teichmann (Capt), A. Venter
British Lions
N. Jenkins, J. Bentley, S. Gibbs, J. Guscott, A. Tait (A. Healey, 78),
G. Townsend, M. Dawson, T. Smith, K. Wood, P. Wallace,
M. Johnson (Capt), J. Davidson, L. Dallaglio, T. Rodber (E. Miller,
78), R. Hill (N. Back, 57)
SCORERS
South Africa
Tries: van der Westhuizen, Montgomery, Joubert
British Lions
Penalty goals: Jenkins (5)
Drop goal: Guscott

Tuesday 1 July
Versus Northern Free State at North West Stadium, Welkom
Won 67–39
TEAMS
Northern Free State
M. Ehrentraut (J. Burrows, 66), R. Harmse, A. van Buuren, T. de
Beer, W. Nagel, E. Herbert, J. Jerling (Capt), K. Appelgryn,
O.Wagener (C. Dippenaar, 78), B. Nel, H. Kershaw, K. Heydenrich,
S. Nieuwenhuysen, E. Delport (A. Michau, 75), M. Venter
British Lions
T. Stimpson, A. Stanger, A. Bateman, N. Beal, T. Underwood,
M. Catt, K. Bracken (A. Healey, 53), J. Leonard (Capt)
(G. Rowntree, 41), M. Regan, D. Young, R. Wainwright,
N. Redman, S. Shaw, N. Back, A. Diprose
SCORERS
Northern Free State
Tries: Ehrentraut, Wagener, van Buuren, Herbert, penalty try
Conversions: Herbert (4)
Penalty goals: Herbert (2)
British Lions
Tries: Underwood (3), Stimpson (2), Shaw (2), Back, Bracken, Regan
Conversions: Stimpson (7)
Penalty goal: Stimpson

Saturday 5 July
Versus South Africa at Ellis Park, Johannesburg
Lost 16–35
TEAMS
South Africa
R. Bennett, A, Snyman, P. Montgomery (H. Honiball, 53), D. van
Schalkwyk, P. Rossouw, J. de Beer, J. van der Westhuizen
(W. Swanepoel, 81), O du Randt (A. Garvey, 63), J. Dalton
(N. Drotske, 69), D. Theron, H. Strydom, K. Otto, J. Erasmus,
G. Teichmann (Capt) (F. van Heerden, 73), A. Venter
British Lions
N. Jenkins, J. Bentley, S. Gibbs, J. Guscott (A. Bateman, 40),
T. Underwood (T. Stimpson, 30), M. Catt, M. Dawson (A. Healey,
81), T. Smith, M. Regan, P. Wallace, M. Johnson (Capt),

J. Davidson, R. Wainwright, L. Dallaglio, N. Back
SCORERS
South Africa
Tries: Montgomery, van der Westhuizen, Snyman, Rossouw
Conversions: de Beer (2), Honiball
Penalty goals: de Beer (3)
British Lions
Try: Dawson
Conversion: Jenkins
Penalty goals: Jenkins (3)

Overall record
Played 13, Won 11, Lost 2, Points For 480, Points Against 278

APPENDIX THREE

Lionised!
The way the press, management and players saw the British Lions matches at the time

Versus Eastern Province Invitation XV
'This game gave us a picture of what we are trying to do. It's all about the right people being in the right place at the right time.'

Ian McGeechan

Versus Border
'The Lions might have hoped to be more at home on a playing surface that oozed water, but Border dominated possession and, with only seven minutes remaining, led by four points. That the Lions then scored eight points to claw back the advantage owed more to superior fitness and a dogged courage than great skill.'

David Hands, *The Times*

Versus Western Province
'Dick Muir and Harry Viljoen, respectively the captain and coach of Western Province, were united in their appreciation of the fast game played by their opponents and, with greater accuracy and better decision-making, the Lions might have scored another four tries.'

David Hands, *The Times*

Versus Mpumalanga
'The British Isles, professional to the core, may regard their afternoon at the Johann van Riebeeck Stadium as a good day at the office. South Africans may take a different view, for victories over Mpumalanga at Witbank are dearly bought and a side that runs in ten tries against them deserves greater respect than the Lions were awarded when their tour began.'

David Hands, *The Times*

Versus Northern Transvaal

'If the Lions had to go down, then it had to be like this: battling to the end and nearly rescuing a cause that, at one stage, looked way, way beyond them. This was a brilliant contest and as the Lions trudged defeated from the battlefield, with the locals of Loftus Versfeld baying with joy over their now-famous victory, it was hard not to admire the manner in which they had very nearly snatched victory from defeat.'

Owen Slot, *The Sunday Telegraph*

Versus Gauteng Lions

'Last Saturday I was very down. I was substituted and I needed a big game. I looked up and saw a hooker in front of me and I'm in trouble if I can't get round a hooker. The full-back was coming across so I had to go inside, but although Austin and I may get the headlines it was the forwards who made it. They were magnificent. I have never seen such elation on the faces of the team members who didn't play as we came off.'

John Bentley

Versus Natal

'Unyielding defence, excellent discipline, the remarkable accuracy of Neil Jenkins' kicking and three tries – for Gregor Townsend, replacement Mike Catt and Lawrence Dallaglio – laid the foundations for a memorable triumph. Natal have never beaten the Lions and rarely in recent years can they have been so comprehensively outplayed.'

Brendan Gallagher, *The Daily Telegraph*

Versus Emerging Springboks

'The British Isles, four days away from the first international of the series with South Africa, achieved everything they could have hoped for in the Boland Stadium here yesterday: a heartening half century of points, no disruptive injuries and the occasional abrupt reminder of the hardness and speed of thought that must be confronted in this country.'

David Hands, *The Times*

First Test versus Springboks

'There is still so much to do, but a fervent spirit now with which to do it. Historically, Test wins by the Lions have always been rare. This was one to savour for years to come.'

Stephen Jones, *The Sunday Times*

Versus Free State Cheetahs

'This was one of the all-time great Lions performances. To come here and play at altitude against one of the top Super-12 teams in a midweek fixture and produce that level of rugby was absolutely outstanding. I'm so proud of them.'

Fran Cotton

Second Test versus Springboks

'Yesterday Durban was claimed for the day by delirious Brits and Irish. After the whistle the whole Lions party, coaches and non-players too, took to the field for a victory parade. It was the day of their lives and the tears and the hugs bore testimony to it.'

Stephen Jones, *The Sunday Times*

Versus Northern Free State

'No touring team should, in my view, be asked to play on a pitch which was rock-hard and where the refereeing is not up to the standards we expect. There were some pretty unsavoury incidents, two or three of stamping on heads, which are totally unacceptable and we will consider taking the appropriate action.'

Fran Cotton

Third Test versus Springboks

'The heavy irony is that this was a more authoritative performance than the second Test win, which sealed the series last week. With less than half their original Test team remaining, and with the rigours of a ferocious season beginning to tell, the Lions gallantly tried to make it a whitewash by spinning the ball all over the field. An heroic effort.'

Stephen Jones, *The Sunday Times*